Children Don't Come with an Instruction Manual

Children Don't Come with an Instruction Manual

A TEACHER'S GUIDE TO PROBLEMS THAT AFFECT LEARNERS

Wendy L. Moss, PhD, ABPP, FAASP

TEACHERS
COLLEGE
PRESS

Teachers College, Columbia University
New York and London

Published by Teachers College Press, 1234 Amsterdam Avenue, New York, NY 10027

Excerpts from the following works reprinted by permission:
  Diagnostic and Statistical Manual of Mental Disorders, Fourth Edition, Text Revision. Copyright © 2000, American Psychiatric Association. Reprinted with permission from the American Psychiatric Association.
  Educational Care: A System for Understanding and Helping Children with Learning Problems at Home and in School by M. Levine. Copyright © 1994. Used by permission of Educators Publishing Service, 625 Mt. Auburn Street, Cambridge, MA, (800)225-5750, www.epsbooks.com.
  Learning Disabilities and Brain Function: A Neuropsychological Approach, 2nd ed, by W. H. Gaddes, 1985, New York: Springer-Verlag. Copyright © 1985 by Springer-Verlag.
  J. Lerner, *Learning Disabilities: Theories, Diagnosis, and Teaching Strategies,* 8th ed., Copyright © 2000 by Houghton Mifflin Company.
  "Annotation: Bullying at School: Basic Facts and Effects of a School Based Intervention Program," by D. Olweus, 1994, *Journal of Child Psychology and Psychiatry,* 35(7), 1171-1190. Used by permission of ACPP Publications.
  Suicide Intervention in the Schools, by S. Poland, 1989, New York: Guilford Press. Used by permission of the publisher.

Library of Congress Cataloging-in-Publication Data

Moss, Wendy, Ph.D.
    Children don't come with an instruction manual : a teacher's guide to problems that affect learners / Wendy L. Moss.
      p. cm.
    Includes bibliographical references and index.
    ISBN 0-8077-4444-1 (cloth) — ISBN 0-8077-4443-3 (pbk.)
    1. Special education.   2. Exceptional children.   I. Title.

LC3965.M69 2004
371.9—dc22   2003063393

ISBN 0-8077-4443-3 (paper)
ISBN 0-8077-4444-1 (cloth)

Printed on acid-free paper
Manufactured in the United States of America

11 10 09 08 07 06 05 04   8 7 6 5 4 3 2 1

To Sarah, Jeremy, and Abigail
and to
all of the other children who have taught me so
much over the years!

Contents

Foreword

It is time that this essential book has been published. There has been an ever-increasing demand on teachers to understand and deal with the well-being of their students. To understand the problems and other situations that can be affecting the child's performance in the school setting, it is now critical for the complete educator to have the tools to identify children in need.

Dr. Moss's book addresses the diverse situations that the teacher may encounter. She addresses everything from learning disabilities, to a child dealing with trauma, to working with the gifted student. This book will facilitate the teacher's ability to consider the individual needs and strengths of atypical children, to improve the input given to the team of educational specialists who will help develop an educational program specific to each child, where indicated, and to make the primary observations and refer, if necessary, to psychologically and medically trained professionals who are best able to help these children with their psychological and medical needs. This book is written in clear and concise language that is easily understood by those who do not have a complete education in psychology, psychiatry, or neurology.

The research for the book is thorough and timely. The author includes quotations garnered from various experts in the field that help to clarify the various situations that she is addressing. In the use of quotations and citations of studies, there is an added depth to the descriptions of the challenges that the teacher and child may experience. She blends the research findings with case studies and with the practical suggestions for teachers. In her final chapter, she presents useful information gathered from students, former students, parents, and experienced teachers as to how they were best helped or were able to help children with learning difficulties, emotional problems, giftedness, and ADHD.

Dr. Moss is uniquely qualified to communicate to teachers an understanding of these problems and how best to deal with them. Both a clinical and a school psychologist, she is the author of several published works in her field and has been recognized as having "advanced competence" in school psychology by the American Board of Professional Psychology.

As a psychiatrist specializing in the treatment of adolescents and adults, and well versed in the dynamics of childhood, I have consulted professionally with Dr. Moss for many years regarding treatment of younger children. I have found her insights to be valuable in the understanding of a child's psychological dynamics. Her understanding of children is profound, as are her approaches to dealing with their problems.

This book offers a necessary contribution to all current teachers and those planning to enter the profession. It is especially important in this twenty-first century, when so many more responsibilities for the child's welfare fall to our teachers.

Donald A. Moses, MD

Preface

As seasoned teachers have observed and new teachers are learning, society seems to be increasing its reliance on educators to guide children through their journey toward becoming emotionally healthy, socially adept, and academically successful adults. Teachers are pressuring themselves to learn more about nonacademic issues so that they can better help their students to develop into well-adjusted, contributing members of society. And media attention leads teachers to impose additional expectations on themselves, as the media raise questions about whether school personnel may be able to identify and prevent violent outbursts, such as those that have caught the attention of the country as children assault and kill other children.

With a packed academic schedule, and the fact that many states have recently adopted new and more rigorous academic standards, it can be difficult for teachers to find time to learn about and identify the multitude of difficulties that their students experience (e.g., emotional, behavioral, social, medical, family, and community stresses). This book provides elementary school educators with an overview of many factors that affect students. This book is a reference manual.

The first chapter reviews the complex nature of understanding and diagnosing children's needs. Chapters 2 through 7 contain information on specific disorders, difficulties, and life stresses that are experienced by students. After obtaining this overview, readers may want to gain further information by reading books and articles that are devoted entirely to the specific topics. Some relevant literature is listed at the end of each chapter.

In the last chapter, students, former students, and parents of challenged youngsters acknowledge how a teacher's actions made a positive difference in their lives. In this same chapter, experienced educators communicate their strategies for assisting children with a variety of needs. The students, parents, and teachers offer viewpoints on how teachers can utilize their personality characteristics and educational strategies to benefit students in classrooms.

Throughout this book, case examples of children who have struggled with specific difficulties, and adults who have tried to help them, are presented to offer a more comprehensive picture of the effect of a disorder or difficulty on youngsters. These case examples represent a composite of many individuals who have had the disorder or challenge and are not representative of any particular student, teacher, or parent. In addition to these case examples, the reader learns about two (fictional) children, Evan and Lisa, who display different symptoms, and how each child may be displaying behaviors because of a variety of possible underlying causes. In other words, their symptoms may be due to a variety of different disorders or stresses. Once an accurate diagnosis is obtained, appropriate interventions can be developed.

This book does not focus on how to teach the academic work. Rather, the goal of this text is to provide information to teachers and prospective teachers who seek to understand how to interpret and respond to children's behaviors, difficulties, and needs.

Acknowledgments

This book was easier for me to write because I received encouragement from so many people. I wish to thank Gloria Moss for her support, for her editorial work, and for giving me her honest opinion about the material. In addition, a special thank-you goes out to two other people: Harold Moss for his support and endless behind-the-scenes practical assistance and Dr. Donald Moses, friend and colleague, who carefully read this manuscript, critiqued it from a professional standpoint, and gave input and support as the project became a reality.

The understanding and consistent availability of the following individuals also allowed me to focus on this project: Donna Goldberg, Penelope Kelley, Dr. Irene Lober, Kenneth Moss, Rebecca Moss, Victoria Ranaldo, and Michael Rubin. In addition, I thank Dr. Noemi Balinth, William Rubin, and my other friends and colleagues who gave me the encouragement I needed in the early stages of this writing project.

Before concluding, I want to acknowledge those exceptional mentors and co-workers with whom I have worked over the years and who have contributed to my knowledge and understanding of children as well as Scott Moss, whose courage and drive to excel had such a significant impact on my life. A heartfelt thank-you to those individuals who selflessly added their personal stories to Chapter 8 because of their desire to help teachers and future students flourish. Last, I want to acknowledge and thank Carol Collins, my editor, and the other staff at Teachers College Press for all their assistance.

CHAPTER 1

Understanding Children

A Complex Exploration

Some children may be exceptionally articulate and speak directly to a trusted teacher about concerns. More often, however, children struggle to identify the source of their distress. I have rarely had an elementary school–aged child enter the office to report that "I'm upset because I think that I have a learning disability." Frequently the child will only be able to state that "I don't understand the work." The student may question his or her intelligence and ability to learn. It is the adults who will need to identify the learning disability, educate the youngster about the challenge, and develop an intervention plan.

At times, students may understand their problems but are hesitant to share this information with others. For instance, one child felt too embarrassed by feelings of anxiety about missing a parent during the schoolday to share her emotional struggle with anyone. Another child had low self-esteem and felt socially isolated but decided that it would not be helpful to share his feelings with others because he believed that no one could help him resolve his social difficulties and feel better.

When children struggle with challenges, they generally communicate with adults, even if it is not in the form of clear, direct statements. The communication is sometimes hard to interpret. Some students speak directly to adults, some communicate through their negative behaviors, others through their overeager style, some through their fear of making mistakes, some through their emotional outbursts, and still others through their level of energy. This book is a reference manual or guide to assist educators in their attempts to understand the messages that their students are sending.

Although it is not the responsibility of the classroom teacher to diagnose children—and it is often not possible to make an accurate diagnosis without conducting a comprehensive assessment of the child's strengths, difficulties, psychosocial influences, developmental history, and so forth—this book offers a concise explanation of many difficulties, obstacles, and challenges that children encounter (e.g., giftedness; learning disabilities; attention-deficit hyperactivity disorder; victimization by bullying; parental divorce). However, it would be quite unusual to find two individuals who show identical symptoms, the identical disorder, the identical severity of the condition, the identical etiology of those symptoms, and the identical response to treatment.

Every human being is influenced by a unique mix of factors, including one's personality, life experience, family factors, intelligence, physiologic influences, and peer interactions. This collection of variables affects how a person reacts to situations, trauma, and other life events as well as how a child communicates distress to others and responds to intervention strategies. Therefore, the individual factors that may affect how a particular student develops and displays a disorder should be kept in mind as information throughout this book is reviewed.

Without a comprehensive assessment of the potential reasons behind a child's symptoms, misinterpretations of a child's difficulties can occur. For instance, a teacher recently remarked that one of her students was clearly spoiled at home. The educator's statement was based on her observation that this student challenged all classroom rules and seemed to believe that he was never responsible for completing his assignments. In another school district, the assistant principal listened to a parent's suspicion that a young classmate of her daughter's might be suffering from abuse at home, since the child never appeared to smile. In yet a third school district, a new student teacher commented to the classroom teacher that a particular child "must have a learning disability," because the child consistently avoided any activity involving reading.

Although the examples of quick judgments cited above are, in my experience, the exception rather than the rule, it is important for teachers to have clear information about childhood issues and to become well versed in identifying the possible symptoms of each difficulty. This knowledge can make it easier for teachers to make educated hypotheses about what might be causing or contributing to student actions and to make referrals for further assessment, when indicated. This book offers specific information about a variety of circumstances and disorders that *may* account for a student's behavior. However, as previously noted, confirmation of a diagnosis often requires a comprehensive, multidisciplinary evaluation. Overt behaviors may not directly point out the underlying cause of the symptoms. Two different case scenarios illustrate this point.

EVAN: A BEHAVIORALLY CHALLENGING SIXTH GRADER

Evan is a sixth-grade student. In December, his teacher, Mrs. Lerner, sought the assistance of the school-based team of specialists, the School Support Team, because she was having difficulty developing a cooperative relationship with Evan. Mrs. Lerner reported that Evan followed classroom rules and expectations during the first few weeks of school, but then his behavior began to gradually deteriorate. Now Evan frequently arrives at class 15 to 20 minutes after the start of school and he greets his classmates in a way that is disruptive to Mrs. Lerner, who is typically teaching a lesson at that time.

Evan does not complete his homework and then laughs at those students who take their work seriously. Mrs. Lerner stated that Evan is sarcastic and often has an "I don't care" attitude about school. She added that Evan socializes with his neighboring classmates, even when they try to ignore him in order to finish their own work. He takes frequent breaks from class to go to the bathroom or to get a drink of water. Mrs. Lerner informed the School Support Team that Evan is currently earning grades of Cs and Ds on his classwork but that she believes he could achieve higher grades if he applied himself.

According to Mrs. Lerner, the most disturbing factor regarding her relationship with Evan is that he directly challenges her authority. For instance, he questions the usefulness of assignments, he does not line up when the children are asked to do so, and he talks during her lessons. Mrs. Lerner added that other staff members (e.g., the science teacher) have similar behavioral concerns when Evan attends their classes.

Before exploring the possible causes of Evan's behaviors, let us first consider a second child's situation.

LISA: A QUIET SECOND GRADER

Lisa is a quiet second-grade student. Mrs. Kane, her teacher, made an appointment with the School Support Team because she was concerned about Lisa's emotional well-being. She explained to the team that "Lisa always seems so sad. She shrugs her shoulders when I ask her what is upsetting her. Lisa will sometimes interact with her peers, but typically she stays to herself. She can be described as a loner. She also has some problems completing her school work, but that's probably because she's too upset to focus on it." After a brief pause, Mrs. Kane added that Lisa follows classroom instructions and is not disruptive.

Could it be possible that Evan and Lisa both suffer from similar concerns? On the surface they seem to be quite different children with very different challenges. Yet there are a variety of problems that could explain both the symptoms presented by Evan and those presented by Lisa.

In order to understand the difficulties that Evan and Lisa may have, there are numerous assessments that can be undertaken to uncover the reason or reasons for their behaviors. Assessment results may reveal that neither child has a serious difficulty or disorder but, rather, that their behaviors were shaped and reinforced by specific events or people in their lives (e.g., Evan's classmates in past years laughed at, and encouraged, some of his statements and actions). However, if one were to assume that a student is just defiant or sullen or energetic, for instance, a child's disorder may be overlooked.

Many disorders include symptoms that also exist in quite different diagnoses, so finding the root of a child's atypical behaviors can be a complex task. The following difficulties are just a few of the possible problem areas with which both Evan and Lisa could be struggling: issues of intelligence (lower than average or higher than average); a learning disability; a language-processing difficulty; medical problems; depression; anxiety/fears/phobias; peer pressure; parent versus teacher expectations; trauma; selection of a dysfunctional role model; family issues; and attention-deficit hyperactivity disorder (ADHD).

Because educators have direct and extended periods of contact with students, they are in an ideal position to identify youngsters who appear to be struggling. Once youngsters are identified, the educator can speak with the appropriate specialists, confer with parents, and learn more about the nature of the child's atypical presentation so that the young student can receive the interventions that are appropriate to allow for academic, social, physical, and emotional growth.

CHAPTER 2

Cognitive and Learning Challenges

Giftedness; Lower than Average IQ;
Learning Disabilities; Language Difficulties

This chapter explores several areas of potential cognitive and learning challenge for students, including issues of intelligence (e.g., giftedness, lower than average IQ), learning disabilities, and language difficulties.

DEFINING INTELLIGENCE

Before exploring how a child's intelligence can affect his or her attitude toward school and academic work, it is important to develop a working definition of *intelligence*. Intelligence is a complex concept that is multifaceted and difficult to define. Yet the term is regularly used in everyday discussions, even among children. I have frequently overheard youngsters making statements to each other about intelligence; for instance, two children comment on another's intellect by offering judgments, such as "He's so stupid" or "She's such a brain."

There are a wide variety of definitions of intelligence (see Gardner, 1999; Goleman, 1995; Neisser et al., 1996). For the purpose of this book, *intelligence* will refer to one's ability to effectively process, organize, and integrate new information and learn from these new data; the ability to analyze new experiences through a divergent thinking style so that various ways of understanding the situations can be hypothesized and assessed; the ability to think in abstract, creative terms; the ability to think convergently; and the ability to understand social communication.

As you know, there are numerous standardized tests of intelligence for both adults and for children (e.g., the Stanford-Binet and Wechsler tests), and these assessment tools typically produce an intelligence quotient, or IQ, score. These scores presume that intelligence is distributed in a bell-shaped curve throughout the population, with most people clustering around the midpoint, or average range. For this discussion, the important point to remember is that

5

an IQ score basically compares a particular individual's test performance with that of others of his or her chronological age. Thus, if a student consistently completes tasks or answers items in a fashion similar to what would be expected of older children, that child would likely attain an IQ score that is above the average range. If another student does not generally perform tasks at a level commensurate with his or her peer group, then that youngster may attain a lower than average IQ score.

Intelligence tests were developed "to measure children's ability to succeed in school" (Neisser et al., 1996, p. 81). Sparrow and Gurland (1998) note that "intelligence tests are currently the best predictor of academic achievement" (p. 60). Neisser and colleagues (1996) concur, commenting that these assessments "do in fact predict school performance fairly well" (p. 81).

There are many areas in which an individual may excel or struggle in comparison to others. Although IQ tests often measure numerous abilities, they do not measure all possible skills. For instance, they may assess one's ability to verbalize factual knowledge and/or one's ability to replicate abstract patterns using blocks or other objects. However, they may not assess one's musical ability, athletic ability, ability to discriminate smells, and many other specific areas of potential competence. This may help to explain why not all children with average IQ scores are found to be average in every area of their lives. In addition, Neisser and colleagues (1996) state that variables apart from intelligence can influence one's school success, "such as persistence, interest in school, and willingness to study" (p. 81). These factors plus a variety of other potentially intervening conditions (e.g., a medical problem, depression, anxiety, environmental deprivation) can lead to decreases in a youngster's display of skills, and overall IQ scores, from one testing session to another.

In sum, although definitions of intelligence vary, the intelligence tests often allow a comparison between an individual and others of the same age on particular ability areas. Test results can give information about how a student might perform academically, but scores can be influenced by a variety of factors, as stated above. Now, how can attaining an IQ score in the gifted range (typically scoring at an overall level in at least the 98th percentile compared to peers) or an IQ score that falls below the average range (typically scoring at an overall level below the 25th percentile compared to peers) lead to unique school challenges?

THE GIFTED CHILD'S SCHOOL DIFFICULTIES

There are many ways in which a child can display giftedness (see Moss, 2002). Specific areas of ability may not be evident in the traditional classroom, such as extraordinary theatrical talent or the ability to cook a gourmet meal. At times, professionals reserve the term *gifted* for those learners who display *numerous* areas of advanced competence. Gifted children who have the ability to understand concepts quickly, generate creative answers, and effectively utilize their areas of talent may thrive in the proper school setting. Such youngsters can gain self-esteem from attaining high grades and teacher praise.

Feldhusen and Moon (1992) note that gifted students often require more "abstract" and "conceptually . . . complex" instruction and lessons than do other students (p. 63). Some gifted students may become bored with traditional academic lessons and begin to "get into trouble" (Gridley, 1987, p. 236). To address gifted students' particular abilities and needs in the classroom, Rohrer (1995) proposes that teachers consider adapting the curriculum, implementing work-study outside of the ordinary classroom program, and teaching "problem solving" with "creative activities" to maximize the diverse ways in which the child can excel (p. 281).

One typical problem that I have noticed with some gifted children is that they have difficulty learning how to learn. The following example illustrates this point.

JESSE: DIFFICULTY LEARNING TO LEARN

Jesse had always been an outgoing, socially successful child who excelled in all academic areas. He quickly grasped concepts and never experienced the need for extra assistance to understand new lessons—that is, until he entered the sixth grade. Jesse's sixth-grade teacher decided to introduce students to the skills required to successfully complete an in-depth research project. Prior to this grade, the students frequently read one or two articles and summarized them in brief reports.

Many of Jesse's classmates asked the teacher for clarification and for an additional review of the information before they started working on the project. Jesse did not seek this guidance. Instead, he left school that day confident that he would understand the assignment once he thought about it. That night, Jesse's parents were concerned because Jesse was in his room crying. When they entered his room, Jesse declared that he must be an "idiot" because he did not know how to proceed with the task. Jesse had never needed and never learned certain skills that his less gifted peers had previously acquired. This included knowing when to ask for assistance, knowing what to do when initial frustration sets in, and knowing that initial difficulty *can* be followed by successful completion of the project. Some gifted students also struggle to overcome their fear that others may no longer view them as bright and gifted if they attempt activities but do not always excel.

LISA AND EVAN: ARE THEY GIFTED?

Going back to our examples of Evan and Lisa, presented in Chapter 1, it is possible that they are both gifted youngsters but lack the patience, or frustration tolerance, to persevere at tasks that they judge to be boring. Lisa was described as a with-drawn youngster. Possibly, she was withdrawing her emotional and intellectual energy from the classroom lessons because she did not view them as challenging. She might have had a preference for, and talent in, drawing and might actually have sat at her desk actively involved in artwork. If Lisa's areas of talent and interest are periodically included into her classroom activities, the teacher may have less diffi-culty engaging her in lessons. Incorporating a youngster's particular skills into the classwork can result in the student becoming less withdrawn and more enthusias-tic about school.

Evan, perhaps, was placed with a teacher who stressed learning of factual data and did not emphasize divergent or creative thinking from students. Evan, then, could have felt unappreciated by his teacher and unclear about the value of the rote exer-cises. His teacher might have been able and willing to adapt certain activities to Evan's specific needs if she had been made aware of them. However, Evan may have inad-vertently hid his needs behind his behavioral disruptions.

ISAAC: THE CLASS CLOWN

Isaac experienced a similar difficulty in his early schooling. His teachers felt that he was an average student who enjoyed being "the class clown." In actuality, Isaac's verbal skills were typical of his peer group, and these skill areas were stressed by his teachers. However, his performance skills (e.g., putting a robot together, fixing bro-ken appliances without direction, taking creative photographs) were far above the levels of children even several years his senior. During a meeting with the school counselor, Isaac was able to articulate his frustration with not having his interests emphasized in school. Isaac's school interest and his grades improved after his teacher agreed to adjust the curriculum to incorporate some of Isaac's more unique abilities; for instance, he made puppets, built a puppet stage, and then used the puppets as a creative method by which to give his history report. Perhaps such academic flexibil-ity would help Evan and Lisa as well.

Suggestions for Teachers Working with Gifted Children: Pros and Cons of Changing the Environment

If a child is gifted but not performing as well as could be expected in class, there are definite benefits that can come from changing the environment to better suit the individual child's needs. However, there are also reasons why educators encourage the child to adapt somewhat to classroom rules and expectations. One reason is that a teacher cannot realistically always foster the ideal environment for a student without depriving another child of at-tention and support. A second reason is that creating different work, sched-uling, or guidelines for the gifted child may create a separation from peers and, potentially, lead to the gifted student feeling isolated. This factor can generally be managed, however, by a sensitive teacher who can monitor how the different academic challenges affect the gifted child's sense of belonging in the class. A third reason that a child is encouraged to learn the skills to adapt to a variety of classroom situations is that these skills may be needed for later success in jobs, relationships, and so on. At times, it can be quite productive to explain these reasons to the gifted student so that he or she understands the logic behind the teacher's decisions.

One must remember that high intelligence does not guarantee success in the world. Rarely, some gifted individuals manage to grow up without needing to adapt to subjectively perceived mundane rules and guidelines determined by others at work. They may, for example, eventually own their own company. However, even these individuals will probably need to develop some frustration tolerance and the ability to concentrate on details that they perceive as boring in order to interact with others in society. Other gifted youngsters will find themselves in jobs where they will have to perform tasks that they do not view as fascinating and will have to realize that the ability to tolerate rote learning may be necessary to succeed (e.g., to get through medical school, to learn computer languages).

Bright but Not Succeeding—Other Explanations

If a teacher or a parent finds that a child is extremely bright but not succeeding in school, it is important to rule out the existence of additional factors that might be hindering academic performance. Factors listed in later chapters should be considered for the gifted youngster who is having trouble, particularly if the teacher has already tried to modify the student's work to allow the child's talents to shine but the difficulties remain. Unfortunately, having high intelligence does not preclude one from suffering from problems such as emotional difficulties, family stresses, learning disabilities, attention-deficit disorders, medical problems, and so on.

If a teacher suspects that a child is unusually bright or talented, it might be advantageous to meet with the student's parents to discuss the pros and cons of offering that youngster more challenging, creative experiences in the areas of strength. Any academic modification should be a positive change for the child and not perceived as a burden or undue pressure. If global giftedness is suspected and hypothesized to be an obstacle to healthy adjustment in the general school program, then the school-based team of specialists, including the school psychologist, might be consulted to determine if administering an IQ test and/or conducting a clinical interview are appropriate steps to take. A psychologist in a mental health clinic or private practice could also perform these assessments; the pros and cons of having evaluations conducted outside the school will be discussed shortly. Once formal and informal evaluations are completed, the possibility of maintaining the child in the traditional school setting versus moving the youngster into a gifted program can be explored by the school personnel and the student's family.

THE STRUGGLES OF THE CHILD WHO HAS
A LOWER THAN AVERAGE IQ

This category includes children with a wide range of abilities. Children with IQ scores that fall approximately within the lowest two percentiles, when raw scores are compared to those obtained from same-aged peers, are sometimes diagnosed as mentally retarded. It is important to note that such a diagnosis assumes a comparatively low IQ but also requires that the youngster have impairments in at least two areas of functioning, such as "deficits in social and adaptive skills" (Crnic & Reid, 1989, p. 248). According to the American Psychiatric Association (APA) (2000), mental retardation involves "significantly subaverage general intellectual functioning . . . that is accompanied by significant limitations in adaptive functioning . . . [and] onset must occur before age 18 years" (p. 41). In addition, the APA indicates that there are four different primary categories of mental retardation, ranging in degree of severity from mildly to profoundly retarded. Individuals who meet the criteria for mental retardation may still display specific areas of strength and weakness.

The child with lower than average intelligence can also be a student whose intelligence, based on IQ scores, falls just below the 25th percentile. The 25th percentile is generally used as a differentiating marker between the low average and average ranges. However, this youngster may actually have average intelligence. Due to a variety of possible influences, such as the error of measurement inherent in an assessment tool, the child's anxiety while taking the test, or the child's atypical background, the achieved score can be below the child's actual cognitive level. A child whose valid IQ score is within the low average range may still have skills in particular areas that are equal to, or even advanced beyond, those of the average peer. For instance, one student had a low average Full Scale IQ and difficulty with most academic work but excelled at expressing his feelings and at batting during baseball season.

Suggestions for Teachers Helping Children
with Lower than Average Intelligence

Youngsters with lower than average intelligence may benefit from extra assistance in school to help them understand topics that are difficult for them (e.g., repetition of lessons; tutoring; multisensory presentations of information, such as the use of verbal and visual cues to stimulate understanding of material). Sometimes students with below-average cognitive skills may not comprehend certain material as easily as peers or they may need more individual attention to master concepts, despite their motivation to succeed. Such children may benefit from the use of hands-on learning (e.g., actual coins to learn about money concepts). Unfortunately, some of these children can be inaccurately labeled as lazy, even by those adults with the best of intentions. When there is no obvious impairment, it can easily appear to teachers or other adults that such a student could grasp the concepts without extra help if he or she were just more motivated.

The most severely impaired children may be candidates for alternative special education programs, day schools, or residential placements; these may be offered outside of the child's current school district. Specialized programs may be beneficial to the child because they can provide specific assistance and training geared toward that youngster's specific needs. However, whenever a child is completely removed from mainstream classes, or leaves his or her home school, the pros and cons of such a decision need to be carefully weighed.

Identifying the Child's Cognitive Strengths and Weaknesses

The identification of a child's cognitive strengths and weaknesses will help adults to better understand the struggling student. The case of Samantha highlights this point.

SAMANTHA: AREAS OF STRENGTH AND WEAKNESS

Samantha was the third child born to highly successful parents. Her older siblings both easily met academic goals. Samantha was socially well accepted and musically inclined. In the early grades, she took pride in her schoolwork, although she often asked her parents or teacher to review or reteach the lessons and concepts. By the fifth grade, however, Samantha began avoiding her schoolwork and commented that "I hate my teacher," "School is stupid," and "I don't need school."

Samantha's fifth-grade teacher and her parents met for a conference to discuss their mutual concerns regarding Samantha's attitude and her minimal academic progress. Initially, they all suspected that Samantha would be able to complete the work easily if only she applied herself. Therefore, they decided to take privileges away from her when she did not complete her schoolwork independently. Two weeks later, her parents and teacher met to review their plan. Samantha had started having temper tantrums at home and often burst into tears in class.

The teacher asked the principal to join this second meeting, because he had known Samantha for several years and might be able to offer additional insights. At this meeting, the principal reviewed his impressions of Samantha's progress and also reviewed the comments that prior teachers had written about Samantha on her report cards. Samantha always appeared to have been a child who responded positively to praise and was interested in gaining additional teacher input before she approached her assignments. Her previous teachers repeatedly stated that Samantha initially seemed to miss certain key aspects of lessons, particularly if they involved new concepts, but that she responded well to more individualized instruction and review.

The principal asked Samantha's parents for permission to have the school-based team of specialists (e.g., reading teacher, educational evaluator, speech pathologist, school psychologist) discuss Samantha's situation and possibly to have the school psychologist and educational specialist assess her intelligence and her academic skills. Samantha's parents, anxious for answers, nervously gave their consent.

Test results suggested that Samantha's intelligence fell within the low average range and that her academic skills were commensurate with her IQ. Assuming that no other factors clouded the validity of the intelligence test results, Samantha's academic progress would need to be assessed in terms of her overall abilities. Her parents were concerned about this feedback initially but agreed that Samantha might, in many areas, just need to have a little more support or different instructions to perform tasks that the average child could complete more easily. Samantha's teacher began to modify certain lessons so that Samantha could continue to learn and to encounter success. In addition, her teacher and parents began supporting and encouraging Samantha's previous adaptive behaviors (e.g., asking for clarification of directions). Samantha's attitude toward school and schoolwork improved dramatically.

Self-Esteem Factors. A lower than average IQ could have led to Evan joking around in class as a way to avoid facing his academic difficulties. It might have caused Lisa to withdraw rather than risk failure. When children with lower than average intelligence are socially aware, their self-esteem can suffer if they feel that they cannot function academically as well as their peers. This lower self-esteem can actually cause them to lose their drive to perform and thus widen the gap between the quality of their schoolwork and that of other students.

Intelligence Tests and Their Interpretation. The interpretation of intelligence tests and IQ scores must be done by professionally trained individuals because a child's future could be negatively impacted by a misunderstanding of scores. For instance, Lisa might have attained an IQ within the low average range. However, she might be severely depressed and therefore have difficulty harnessing the energy to complete the tasks. Her IQ, without the depression impacting the results, might have been considerably higher. If her teacher or parents had simply lowered academic expectations based on test results, there might have been a delay in arranging for Lisa to get help for her emotional difficulties. In addition, Lisa might have inaccurately concluded that she was less academically competent than her peers, since the adults no longer held her accountable for the same level of work. This interpretation might have exacerbated depressive symptoms (e.g., low self-esteem) and could have produced a cycle of increased depression leading to decreased school grades, leading to more modifications of work, resulting in yet another increase in the depression. Work modifications might be a beneficial intervention for certain children, under certain circumstances, but if the student has negative emotional responses, then this reaction would need to be addressed.

After administering an IQ test, the trained evaluator assesses the intra-subtest and inter-subtest scatter in the results. At times, significant scatter may raise questions about whether the student has a learning disability in the areas that are relatively weak. The lower scores and the higher scores can also be important information for better understanding the child as a learner. The gifted child may have relative weaknesses that could benefit from intervention, and the child with a lower than average IQ score may have some advanced skills that could be fostered.

Success—It Takes More than Intelligence

Some children with lower than average intelligence are more successful in life than some children with stronger cognitive skills. Youngsters who are able to verbalize their confusion about tasks, are able to ask for assistance, are motivated to succeed, and persevere when frustration mounts have important tools needed for success. A child who has academic difficulties due to cognitive or other struggles (e.g., a learning disability or a language difficulty) may do quite well in suitable jobs that tap areas of relative strength. Without the drive to succeed, it is hard to be successful in any career.

School, like life, is not only for the average child. The experienced teacher routinely assumes that children will enter the class with varying levels of intelligence. Teachers have the complex challenge of trying to offer curricula to students in such a way that the child with lower than average intelligence can conquer the task demands while the child with higher than average intelligence can also be cognitively enriched by the lessons. For example, one child may be expected to study an aspect of a country by reviewing an article with some assistance, while another child may be asked to independently read a few articles and then search the Internet for more in-depth information about another aspect of the country. If varying the work does not create a negative sense of grouping, it may be an appropriate intervention. Each teacher will need to decide how to meet the varying needs of students.

There are times, however, when a child deviates significantly from the average range (i.e., the mentally retarded child or extremely gifted child) and may benefit from work with another faculty member (e.g., a specialist in the school building) or an alternative program. In less extreme cases, the teacher might consider consulting with the school-based team of specialists, since some of the team members may be trained to help modify the curriculum based on a particular student's needs. Recommendations for students who are at the extremes of the bell-shaped curve on the intelligence tests should be reviewed on a case-by-case basis by the school staff, the parents, and, at times, by the Committee on Special Education.

When teachers and parents want to clarify a child's cognitive skill profile, they may decide to seek an IQ evaluation by a qualified psychologist. This assessment may be performed within the school setting, particularly if the school staff feels that it would be important to gain this information in order to develop a more successful academic or social environment for the student. Or, as noted earlier, parents may choose to ask a psychologist outside the school system to complete the evaluation. This latter option is sometimes selected by parents because they trust a particular psychologist in the community or they seek to increase the privacy of the process. When testing is completed outside the school, however, there is a fee for the evaluation and the child may feel less comfortable in unfamiliar surroundings than when the assessment is conducted in the child's own school. I have noted that parents generally decide to share the privately completed evaluation with the school psychologist when the information could potentially help the school staff to better understand and assist the student.

The psychologist will need to weigh the pros and cons of administering an IQ test to referred children. The numerous benefits (e.g., determining cognitive strengths and weaknesses, potentially determining a child's intelligence, helping to determine whether a learning disability is present) need to outweigh the risks (e.g., having parents or teachers inappropriately change their perceptions of the child, having parents or teachers believe that the IQ is unaffected by other factors such as a child's depression; having the child question "Is something wrong with me?" because he or she is undergoing the evaluation). I support the administration of IQ tests when there is a clear reason for obtaining the score and after the evaluator has considered whether other assessments, such as emotional and behavioral evaluations, are indicated to more fully understand the factors influencing the IQ score and the child's overall level of functioning.

In summary, intelligence testing can provide useful information about individuals, but these scores need to be evaluated carefully with the understanding that IQ tests provide only a specific range of data about the total child. It is important to maintain a holistic view of the youngster while gradually narrowing down the root or roots of the school struggles. There are some children who appear to have lower than average intelligence but actually suffer from other difficulties, such as learning disabilities, language-processing difficulties, environmental deprivation, anxiety, depression, or even medical problems. In addition, a child who views his or her cognitive skills as being somewhat weaker than average may develop secondary symptoms (e.g., low self-esteem) that need to be identified and addressed.

LEARNING DISABILITIES

Learning disabled (LD) children are not a homogeneous group. In fact, these youngsters can have IQ scores anywhere along the continuum from gifted through the lower than average ranges. The learning disabled student may have difficulty in one skill area or in several. The one thing that these children have in common, however, is that their performance or aptitude on specific skills is not equal to their typical ability levels in other areas.

Defining Learning Disabilities

Gaddes (1985) explains that the mentally retarded student scores relatively low on cognitive and neuropsychological assessments and that these scores are fairly evenly distributed within a narrow range, while the learning disabled child will show more scatter, reflecting more discrepancies between areas of strength and weakness. The American Psychiatric Association (2000) states that "learning disorders are diagnosed when the individual's achievement . . . in reading, mathematics, or written expression is substantially below that expected for age, schooling, and level of intelligence" (p. 49) and that this difficulty interferes with adaptive functioning (e.g., completing schoolwork).

Given these brief glimpses at definitions, many individuals seem to have a learning disability. However, not all learning struggles indicate the presence of a learning disability. For instance, when Eddie first moved to America he was unable to comprehend the material in English-language books due to a lack of experience with the language. His inability to read the books significantly impacted his performance in school. Eddie, however, did not suffer from a learning disability or disorder. He just needed training to overcome the temporary obstacle. In the definition quoted earlier from the American Psychiatric Association (2000), it was noted that the student's difficulty would need to be unexpected given his or her educational experiences. In Eddie's case his English reading skills *were* commensurate with his limited training in this subject area.

The Research

There have been a wide variety of definitions of *learning disabilities*, perhaps explaining why there have also been a wide variety of estimates regarding the incidence of learning disabilities among populations of children. However, it is estimated that about 5 percent of students are diagnosed as having a learning disability (APA, 2000) or as needing assistance due to a learning disability (Lerner, 2000) in school.

Lerner (2000) indicates that although there are numerous ways in which learning disabilities are defined, there are often common features, including the following:

(1) central nervous system dysfunction,
(2) uneven growth pattern and psychological processing deficits,
(3) difficulty in academic and learning tasks,
(4) discrepancy between achievement and potential, and
(5) exclusion of other causes. (p. 10)

"The exact causes of learning disabilities are largely unknown" (Taylor, 1989, p. 348), and there is not one blood test or medical evaluation that can identify the root of all forms of learning struggles (Lerner, 2000). In some situations, however, specific medical issues can be identified as causing or contributing to the learning difficulties (e.g., brain injury). In these cases, professionals can utilize their knowledge about the specific organic site of difficulty to create an educational intervention plan. Gaddes (1985), for instance, notes that if "a child has difficulty learning the alphabet because of a left-hemisphere dysfunction, he may be taught by singing" (p. 17).

Experienced special educators and classroom teachers, aware of the fact that there can be more than one way to teach a concept, may present alternative learning strategies when the initial teaching of the lesson is not effective for the struggling and/or learning disabled student. These strategies can be developed based on the child's learning style and pattern, even when there is no diagnosed organic impairment. Mainstream classroom teachers might collaborate with the child's special education teacher to develop appropriate instruction for a classified student while addressing the goals for the class.

A learning disabled child can have one or more deficits or areas of challenge. Taylor (1989) reports that deficits may include "speech and language, visual-perceptual skills, sensory-motor abilities, use of cognitive strategies, and . . . memory, reasoning, and attentional capacities" (p. 348). These underlying weaknesses may cause deficits to emerge as a youngster approaches certain academic tasks. The American Psychiatric Association (2000) identifies four primary learning disorders: "Reading Disorder" (p. 51), "Disorder of Written Expression" (p. 54), "Mathematics Disorder" (p. 53), and a "Learning Disorder Not Otherwise Specified" (p. 56). This section briefly explores the first three of these areas. Deficits in some language-based processes are examined later in the chapter.

When reviewing the following disability categories, a note of caution is needed. Children are not born with an innate developmental clock that is synchronized to the exact timetable of the next child. Therefore, there is some normal variability to when children master certain skills. Significant delays, however, or lack of progress in an area might warrant further investigation.

Reading Disabilities

This area of learning disability, sometimes referred to as dyslexia, is "the most common type of learning disability" (Shaywitz, Fletcher, & Shaywitz, 1995, p. S50). Lerner (2000) states that "at least 80 percent" of learning disabled students "encounter difficulties in reading" (p. 386). Many investigators have proposed definitions for various forms of reading struggles. For instance, Shaywitz and colleagues (1995) describe dyslexia as "a core deficit in a particular component within the language system (phonologic processing)" (p. S51). Pennington (1991) describes dyslexia as a "difficulty in learning to read and spell . . . [where] there is no obvious reason for the difficulty, such as inadequate schooling, peripheral sensory handicap, acquired brain damage, or low overall IQ" (pp. 45–46). Gaddes (1985) suggests that "many educators use the term 'alexia' to indicate a complete or very severe inability to read, and 'dyslexia' to mean a mild dysfunction or moderate retardation in reading" (p. 276). Gaddes adds, however, that this differentiation of terms has not been universally adopted.

Reading is a complicated process that involves the simultaneous use of a variety of skills. Adults often read with such automatic fluency that it is difficult to remember the challenge of integrating all the different facets of the reading process. Levine (1994) gives a detailed description of many of the subprocesses needed to attain successful reading skills. This list is presented here not for memorization but rather for teachers to perhaps gain a deeper appreciation of the reading tasks presented to new learners. According to Levine (1994), reading primarily involves eight subprocesses:

(1) *Phonological awareness*— . . . [the ability to] make fine distinctions between individual language sounds . . .
(2) *Paired association memory*—the formation in memory of a strong bond between a particular letter or group of letters and a language sound . . .

(3) *Visual processing and pattern recognition*—the ability to appreciate the distinct visual characteristics of individual letters and whole words and to label them accurately . . .

(4) *Active working memory*—the capacity to take apart and/or put together the sounds within a word . . . [which involves] the capacity to hold the component sounds in active working memory . . .

(5) *Semantic facility*—rapid access to the stored meanings of words . . .

(6) *Automatization*—the simultaneous and automatic occurrence of all of the above operations . . .

(7) *Sentence comprehension*—the ability to derive meaning from the structure of sentences . . .

(8) *Discourse comprehension*—the interpretation of reading beyond the sentence level. (pp. 161–162)

Sternberg and Grigorenko (2002) explored criteria for defining reading disabilities and do not support the use of a discrepancy approach (discrepancy between one's reading level and one's intelligence) to determine which youngsters need reading assistance. Rather, they assert that it is important only to identify where the problem in reading lies and teach according to the child's needs.

Reading difficulties may be related to a weakness in one or more of the underlying processes. The ability to connect sounds and symbols (letters) can involve both language skills and visual-perceptual skills. In addition, memory issues and the ability to focus on the small details of printed words can affect one's rate of reading acquisition. Pennington (1991) states that the major deficit apparent in those with reading disabilities is in the area of their "phonological processing skills" (p. 58). He notes that other professionals have proposed alternative explanations, such as "faulty eye movements, vestibular system dysfunction, general problems in rule-learning or conceptual skills, differential sensitivity to certain light frequencies, failure of binocular convergence, . . . and so on" (p. 58). Pennington adds, however, that "none of these other, sometimes esoteric, explanations of dyslexia enjoy anything like the empirical support that the language-processing explanation and corresponding treatments do" (p. 58). For an individual child, though, the specific type of reading errors and struggles will need to be evaluated so that the specialist can assess the underlying weakness, or weaknesses, and develop intervention strategies.

As discussed, reading is not a simple act. Because of this, special educators do not develop identical intervention plans for all children diagnosed as having a reading disability. One child may have a particular weakness in a facet of memory while another youngster may have intact memory skills but visual-perceptual deficits. Treatment plans typically work to build on a child's areas of strength while addressing specific weaknesses.

GEORGE: READING STRUGGLES

George's second-grade teacher became concerned about his apathy toward reading. She was unsure whether George was uninterested in reading but capable of mastering the task or whether he was struggling with the skill and, as a result, became frustrated, unmotivated, and uninterested. George would frequently wander around the room or try to distract peers during reading periods. His parents also reported that George was reluctant to engage in reading tasks at home.

A psychologist evaluated George and found that his overall intelligence was within the average range. An educational specialist found that his reading skills were significantly below expected levels for a second-grade student. The educational specialist also reported that he had difficulties with his short-term retention of certain material. This difficulty could possibly explain why George seemed to unlearn or forget reading lessons taught on previous schooldays (e.g., the connection between letters and sounds) when he returned to his reading group for additional skill-building activities. The speech-language pathologist also tested George and found that he had difficulty discriminating certain sounds from one another. This could cause him to have trouble identifying the differences between letter sounds and could make reading a more stressful process. All three evaluators reported that George was animated and appeared to be motivated during testing sessions.

George's parents and teacher were notified of all test results. It was recommended that he be given the opportunity to attend the specialized learning program within the school. This program allowed him to receive small-group instruction briefly each day. The school district's Committee on Special Education identified George as having a learning disability and developed an Individualized Education Plan (IEP) for him. This plan gave his special education teacher, parents, and, when appropriate, George himself a clearer explanation of the goals of the program and methods to be utilized to reach them.

George's IEP described how his strengths would be emphasized, to build his self-confidence and reading skills, while specific strategies would be employed to help improve his areas of deficit. Some of the confidence-building lessons that were employed for George included offering him books at a level that he was able to master; presenting him with pattern books to help him to temporarily retain the repeated sentence patterns in the book once he grasped the initial pattern; helping him understand that he already had some reading skills (e.g., he could read his name and some other high-frequency words in his books, such as I); and helping him understand that he was already capable of connecting visual symbols (e.g., a stop sign) to meaning so that now the process of connecting a string of letters to meaning was just the next step.

George's areas of difficulty were addressed through work with both the special education teacher and the speech-language pathologist. Initially, both specialists developed game-oriented drills for George. As he became more engaged in the process, they began to focus more directly on reading activities. Both specialists also gave suggestions to George's classroom teacher and his parents on ways to encourage George's reading behaviors without entering into power struggles with him.

If a teacher or a parent suspects that a child suffers from a reading disability, the school's team of specialists may be able to offer suggestions on how to proceed. Testing could highlight the child's overall abilities and patterns of strength and weakness. When there is suspicion of a neurological or physiological cause of reading problems (e.g., poor vision, concentration deficits, memory impairment), the school team may recommend a medical evaluation to ensure that such difficulties are not overlooked.

Not all children with reading difficulties need assistance through the special education department. For instance, Eddie was the youngster described earlier who struggled with reading English texts because he had recently moved to America and was just beginning to master the language. This student needed some assistance but, since he could read Spanish fluently, was probably not reading disabled. Eddie's school district arranged for him to meet with a specialist several times each week until his grasp of the language improved enough to allow him to more fully and independently process information within his regular classroom setting. Within a few months, his teacher was impressed with his skill acquisition and Eddie was discharged from extra help. In some school districts, Eddie might have been enrolled in a special program for children who are in the process of learning English.

Learning Disability in Written Expression

There are many books written entirely about various forms of learning disabilities. One category of disability is sometimes referred to as a written language or written expression learning disability.

The American Psychiatric Association (2000) notes that a "Disorder of Written Expression" (p. 56) may be present if a student's "writing skills . . . are substantially below those expected given the person's chronological age, measured intelligence, and age-appropriate education" (p. 56) and if the skill deficit hampers adaptive functioning (e.g., ability to complete schoolwork).

A disability in the area of written expression could involve struggles in specific components of the writing task, such as handwriting skill and the use of language in written work. Lerner (2000) comments:

> Competent writing requires many related abilities, including facility in spoken language, the ability to read, skills in spelling, legible handwriting or skill with computer keyboarding, knowledge of the rules of written usage, and cognitive strategies for organizing and planning the writing. (p. 443)

In each task, multiple demands are placed upon the child. For instance, Gaddes (1985) reports that handwriting involves "visual scanning, right-left orientation, sequencing, motor development, spatial imagery, visual-motor coordination, visual form recognition, and all or most of the complexities of speech and language development" (p. 228). If the child's only weakness in the area of written expression is related to the muscle control necessary to create legible handwriting, this problem is sometimes separated into a category known as a "Developmental Coordination Disorder" (APA, 2000, p. 56).

Gaddes (1985) describes three general "processes" related to "oral and written language":

(1) *Phonological processing*. . . . the recognition and muscular-motor production of language or phonetic sounds.
(2) *Semantics*. The understanding of the meaning of single words . . . [and]
(3) *Syntax*. The systematic arrangement of words in a meaningful sentence structure. (pp. 253–254)

Another explanation of the writing process is postulated by Levine (1994). He states that writing involves the ability for "encoding thoughts into words, sentences, and discourse," the ability to use one's muscle groups to write, the ability to remember the needed skills for writing tasks, "attention to details," "self-monitoring," utilizing various "strategies while writing," "organization," the ability for "generation of thoughts," "reading ability," "enjoyment of writing," the ability to write for another person—the reader—and the ability to edit one's own work (pp. 182–184).

After reviewing this information about the numerous processes involved in developing effective written language skills, teachers may develop a new appreciation for the child's journey toward task mastery. Sometimes parents need to be educated as well so that they do not become too frustrated or impatient if they find imperfections in their youngster's written work. It is a complicated process that takes encouragement from others, motivation from within, and guidance.

WILLIAM: DIFFICULTY ORGANIZING WRITTEN WORK

One child, William, loved to draw and write. He had many areas of strength in his writing-related skills. He had a wealth of ideas, his handwriting was age-appropriate, and his vocabulary and ability to verbally describe scenes were well developed. Yet his peers and many adults had difficulty understanding his written stories. William had enormous difficulty with his written organization of thoughts. He might start in the middle of a story, then jump around from beginning to end before completing the written piece with a reference to an event that he had not previously described. William, after receiving psychological, educational, and speech-language evaluations, was not determined to have severe enough relative weaknesses to be classified as learning disabled. However, he received extra support to learn ways to help himself to outline and organize his stories so that readers could enjoy his written efforts. William was responsive to the intervention and slowly began to improve the organization of his writings. He was pleased when readers were able to easily process his plot without asking him numerous clarifying questions.

Spelling Disability

Another component of written language has to do with spelling. According to Pennington (1991), "when we read, we go from letters to phonological representations, and when we spell, we go from phonological representations to letters" (p. 60).

Levine (1994) describes the multiple steps involved in spelling:

(1) *Phonological encoding*—the ability to represent English language sounds with appropriate letter combinations . . .
(2) *Graphemic retrieval*—the ability to recall the visual configurations of words . . .
(3) *Segmentation*—the ability to take apart words and put them back together again . . .
(4) *Rule recall*—the ability to . . . remember rules governing spelling . . .
(5) *Attention to detail* . . .
(6) *Semantic networking and appreciation of morphology*—an awareness of how words relate to their meanings, their roots, and their common derivations . . .
(7) *Retrieval memory*—access to stored spellings . . . [and]
(8) *Reading ability*—strong word decoding skills. (pp. 176–177)

Written language deficits, whether due to spelling errors or other problems, can create frustration on the part of students who question why others fail to, or struggle to, understand their attempts at written communication. Asking the child to try harder may only increase that youngster's frustration. When a child is truly learning disabled, that student may require alternative ways to master the skills rather than simply spending more time practicing the original method of learning. This is where the training of special education evaluators and specialists can be extremely helpful. They may be able to determine, for instance, whether a child with significant handwriting difficulties should learn keyboarding skills or, perhaps, should learn another method of improving handwriting and completing written assignments. Occupational therapists may also provide insight as to whether a child's motor skill functioning is affecting handwriting. For some students, the occupational therapist or learning specialist may prefer to avoid encouraging full reliance on keyboarding if the student is assessed to be capable of attaining functional handwriting after further guided practice.

The specialist may also be able to offer an opinion about whether a spell-check computer program would be appropriate for a particular child. Many factors need to be considered. For instance, would the child become so reliant on the computer that he or she would not make an effort to learn the rules and skills needed to spell when no computer is available? Would the computer even be helpful? Many computer programs still require the user to select the proper spelling from a list—could the child master this task? In addition, some words may not be identified by a computer program as being misspelled. For instance, Nate typed "Witch one of the bad guys got shoot?" and was rewarded by the computer's lack of identification of his spelling errors (he ignored the computer feedback about his grammatical errors, since this was not his focus of concern). Nate later became frustrated when his teacher circled *witch* and *shoot* as being misspelled words.

Mathematics Disorder

Some students have a learning disability in the area of mathematics (APA, 2000; Lerner, 2000). The diagnostic criteria are similar to those identified for other learning disorders, with the exception that the skill deficit falls within the area of mathematics. At times, teachers may notice that children with reading disabilities begin to struggle in the area of math as well. This occurrence may not be due to underlying mathematics deficits but rather to the increased use of language in mathematics word problems. Lerner (2000) reports that approximately one-quarter of all students with a learning disability receive support to help them in the area of mathematics.

Levine (1994) describes specific tasks required to succeed in mathematics. Mathematics involves the use of memory skills, "visual processing," "conceptualization" skills, the ability to understand the "use of language in a mathematical context," "problem-solving skills," and "mathematical comfort and affinity" (pp. 200–201).

CHARLES: VISUAL-SPATIAL DIFFICULTIES

Sometimes a child's problems can be solved easily. Charles was a third-grade student who could typically multiply, add, and subtract numbers in his head. Yet he frequently arrived at wrong answers when he was required to write the numbers and complete the mathematical process on paper. His errors were frequently due to visual-spatial difficulties. He did not line up numbers correctly or carried numbers over two places instead of one. Charles eventually began using graph paper; with this intervention, he was able to compensate for his area of weakness.

Suggestions for Teachers: Working with the LD Child

When a child has an area of disability, concrete and practical lessons may be beneficial. For instance, a child who has trouble conceptualizing mathematical facts may benefit from using manipulatives (i.e., objects) to show how 10 minus 4 equals 6. A child who has deficits in determining the difference between a *b* and *d* may benefit from a hand game in which the left hand can form a *b* and the right hand can form a *d*. Sometimes a little note on a child's desk may be a temporary but useful guide for clarifying spelling rules.

While children are taught the purpose of learning to read, write, and perform mathematical equations in class, parents might be encouraged to reinforce the value of these subjects at home. In fact, an educator may gently remind parents that they can encounter opportunities to authentically teach some lessons outside of the school hours. For instance, if a child asks questions about a particular subject of interest, the parent can borrow a book from the library, and both child and parent can learn together. Initially, or if the book is too complex, the parent might want to do all the reading. As a child's skill level and confidence improve, the child may be encouraged to help read certain sections or read it entirely and then review the information and share impressions with a parent.

When a child wants to purchase an item, the parent may use this situation to review mathematical concepts; for example, if Steve has 20 cents and wants to buy a small item for 25 cents, how much money does he still have to obtain? If Steve understands the applied purpose of mathematics, it may help him appreciate the classroom lessons rather than just viewing them as busywork. These examples highlight the need for continued parent–teacher cooperation.

There are many tools that can be used to help learning disabled children improve in, or compensate for, their areas of weakness. It is often advantageous to the child when the parents, classroom teacher, and special educators coordinate efforts so that the child receives one consistent intervention approach and does not feel overwhelmed or confused by conflicting approaches to, or excessive emphasis on, deficits.

Children need to spend time focusing on areas of strength, even while they receive remediation for areas of weakness. This may seem obvious, but sometimes it's important to restate the obvious. Taylor (1989) reports that students with learning disabilities should be encouraged to pursue extracurricular activities that tap into their areas of strength. Taylor feels that the result of such activity can be an improved self-image and self-assuredness; concurrently, the children will have the opportunity to reduce the tension that may build when they engage in academically oriented schoolwork. As stated in the previous chapter, we need to view children holistically and help them develop into emotionally healthy, happy individuals who are prepared for the overall challenges of life. If disabilities are not addressed, this may cause frustration later in life, but, conversely, overemphasizing disabilities may lead a child to believe that he or she has few areas of ability.

If we return to our scenarios involving Evan and Lisa, originally described in Chapter 1, they both may be responding behaviorally (i.e., Evan by acting out and Lisa by withdrawing) to feelings of inadequacy either because of unidentified learning disabilities or because of an overemphasis on their areas of disability. They may believe that they are less capable than their peers—so why compete? If this perception exists, then both Evan and Lisa may need some education about their area of disability so they know that having a specific learning disability does not equal having a lack of intelligence or lack of ability in other areas. Readers might want to keep in mind that even if Evan and Lisa have identified abilities as well as learning disabilities, based on test results, they may still have other difficulties (e.g., language-processing problems, depression, anxiety, family problems) that affect school functioning. The diagnostic process is complicated and takes time if the evaluators want to gain a thorough and accurate picture of the one factor, or multiple factors, impacting a child.

LANGUAGE DEFICITS CAN IMPACT LEARNING

Language, the means by which people communicate with one another, can include a broad spectrum of skills and methods. For instance, some individuals successfully communicate using traditional verbal language, while others use sign language, body language, written language, or a combination of these. This section examines some childhood difficulties and school challenges that can result from deficits in various underlying processes of verbal communication. Verbal communication involves two major components—expressive language and receptive language. The first has to do with one's ability to communicate thoughts or feelings to others, while the latter has to do with one's ability to successfully comprehend the language of others.

Lahey (1988) describes language disorders as those that leave an individual with language deficits in "the learning or use of one's native language" when his or her language functioning level is compared to that of other people of the same age (p. 21).

Expressive Language Deficits

Expressive language deficits may involve characteristics such as

> a limited amount of speech, limited range of vocabulary, difficulty acquiring new words, word-finding or vocabulary errors, shortened sentences, simplified grammatical structures, limited varieties of grammatical structures (e.g., verb forms), limited varieties of sentence types (e.g., imperatives, questions), omissions of critical parts of sentences, use of unusual word order, and slow rate of language development. (APA, 2000, p. 59)

Many children with areas of expressive language difficulties can still be successful communicators because they effectively compensate for their areas of weakness. For instance, a 5-year-old girl often emphasized body language and facial expressions to help the listener understand her needs. Her teacher noticed that most of this student's questions were in the form of a single word. For instance, she might ask for crayons by saying "Crayons?" while simultaneously displaying a puzzled facial expression. Her parents were aware of her "dramatic body language" but did not realize that underlying language deficits may have led this child to overemphasize these nonverbal abilities. Informal information gathering, such as classroom observations or obtaining a developmental history from the parents, and formal evaluations, such as administering standardized tests, can help a speech-language pathologist determine whether such a youngster has delayed language skills.

Word-Finding Deficits. Word-finding deficits, a specific expressive language concern, involve difficulty finding the particular word or words to describe thoughts. These word-finding, or word-retrieval, problems can sometimes cause hesitation or delays in a child's speech as he or she searches for the desired word. This pattern of hesitation or response delay, if present, may mislead a teacher into believing that a child is simply extremely shy or self-conscious rather than struggling with an underlying language issue. However, it is also true that uncertainty and insecurity can actually become a secondary problem for these children as they become aware of their area of language weakness.

Not all children suffering from word-finding deficits exhibit the same expressive language characteristics, such as hesitations, nor do their areas of difficulty follow only one pattern. For instance, some children can speak fluently and struggle with word-retrieval issues only in specific situations (e.g., when asked to label a picture or retrieve a word in isolation). An example may help to clarify this point. Ron was a first-grade student who was social and verbal. Unlike some other language-impaired youngsters, he could easily communicate his needs. However, when asked to name objects in pictures, he struggled. Ron was unable to tell his teacher that a specific picture was of a clock, yet he was able to report that "that thing, it tells time, the clock goes on the wall." While describing the object, Ron was able to state that it was a "clock," yet he had previously been unable to recall the name without this added context.

As previously noted, some children interrupt their spontaneous dialogue when they are unable to recall a specific word. I have witnessed this pattern in numerous children, who state, "I forgot how you say it" or "What is that word again?" Some students may use general terms, such as "that thing." At times, this interruption of expressive language might subject the child to peer ridicule or teacher impatience. If a language-impaired youngster experiences this added stress, then anxiety or increased self-consciousness can exacerbate the initial word-finding difficulties.

EVAN AND LISA: LANGUAGE DEFICITS?

Let us return to our two case examples, Evan and Lisa. On the surface, we might rule out an expressive language disorder as the cause of Evan's behavioral difficulties. After all, his teacher found that he talked frequently, maybe even too frequently in certain situations. Frequency of verbalizations should not be the guideline by which a child is, or is not, considered to have a possible language disorder. In fact, if Evan suffers from a word retrieval problem, he may "circumlocute, or talk around the idea [that he is] . . . trying to communicate" (Lahey, 1988, p. 27). This can result in increased verbalizations due to a lack of efficiency in communicating succinctly. If his teacher, upon questioning, recognizes that Evan appears to have difficulty concisely expressing ideas or sometimes expresses them awkwardly, then a speech-language pathologist may want to determine whether a language-related deficit is present.

Our other case example, Lisa, was withdrawn and minimally verbal in class. A child who has trouble generating words to accurately communicate ideas may become self-conscious and withdrawn. As noted earlier, a teacher who does not allow an individual, such as Lisa, to have extra time to verbalize thoughts, or students who begin to tease the child because of delayed verbal responses, may exacerbate this student's stress.

Selective Mutism. There are some students who may not talk at all or may verbalize thoughts only rarely while they are at school. This behavior does not necessarily suggest the existence of a language disorder. Selective mutism is a disorder that reflects a child's "persistent failure to speak in specific social situations" (APA, 2000, p. 125) despite intact abilities to communicate verbally. Such youngsters may speak easily but only in certain classes, such as in gym class but not in music class, or they may be mute throughout the schoolday (see Chapter 7). The school psychologist and school speech-language pathologist should consult one another if a child is suspected of having selective mutism to determine whether emotional or language diffi-culties are the primary basis of the problem. Some language-disordered chil-dren may limit verbalizations because of their awareness of their language weaknesses, but the primary diagnosis would not be selective mutism for these students.

Other Manifestations of Language Struggles. There are numerous expres-sive language areas that speech-language pathologists assess. Some speech and language concerns not previously mentioned in this section but that parents and teachers might encounter include dysfluency, quality-of-voice difficulties (e.g., hoarseness), unusual or inappropriate uses of words, motor difficulties involving the speech area, and articulation errors. Children with significant psychiatric conditions, such as autism or psychotic disorders, may display other atypical language. For instance, a child may have echolalia (i.e., repeating back verbatim statements made by others), may display frequent word or sentence repetition, or may verbalize strings of words or ideas that lack clear meaning or have unusual meanings.

Receptive Language Deficits

Let us now examine the second major component of verbal communication, *receptive language*. Receptive language difficulties affect one's accuracy in understanding another's communication. This can be caused by many fac-tors. "Because the development of expressive language in childhood relies on the acquisition of receptive skills, a pure receptive language disorder . . . is virtually never seen" (APA, 2000, p. 62).

Understanding the verbal statements of others depends, in part, on a child's ability to hear or lip-read the words. Although complete deafness is often easily diagnosed before the child reaches school age, milder forms of hearing loss can be more difficult to identify. For instance, Lahey (1988) notes that children can have temporary hearing loss as a result of periodic ear in-fections. Therefore, depending on the time of the hearing test, the child may or may not be found to suffer hearing loss. Allergies and other medical dif-ficulties that cause congestion of the ear–nose–throat region can also inter-fere with a student's ability to hear.

If a child has trouble hearing the teacher, that student may find school frustrating and tune-out or act-out. Similarly, if a child can adequately hear but has deficits in the processing of the auditory information, then similar emotional and behavioral problems can emerge. Receptive language difficul-ties may include "difficulty understanding words, sentences, or specific types of words . . . and deficits in various areas of auditory processing" (APA, 2000,

p. 62). Moss and Sheiffele (1994) note that "auditory processing skills range from simple sound localization and discrimination to the multi-faceted task of comprehending complex language structures. Deficiencies can occur in varying degrees in any of these areas" (p. 89). These authors also note that deficits in verbal memory skills may impact one's receptive language abilities.

MICHELLE: LANGUAGE STRUGGLES

Let us examine a few of the factors that can hamper a child's ability to process auditory input. Some children, like Michelle, struggle with deficits in their figure–ground skills. Michelle could not efficiently filter out extraneous sounds, such as other students whispering or the noise generated when pages in books are turned, as she tried to attend to her teacher's lesson. Adults sometimes experience figure–ground difficulties when they try to talk with a friend at a party, struggling to isolate their friend's words from the other noises in the room.

Michelle also had difficulty in the area of auditory closure, which involves being able to fill in missing sounds. Many students can accurately guess at the word a teacher used even though one of the syllables was mumbled or a child dropped a book while the word was being spoken. Youngsters like Michelle, who have difficulty with this skill and/or with discriminating two similar-sounding words, may struggle with the processing of some auditory information.

Michelle suffered from moderate central auditory–processing deficits. She was able to grasp spoken language when her teacher explained concepts or ideas to her in a quiet, small-group context or one on one. However, large-group lessons often resulted in Michelle feeling "dumb," saying "I can't get it," or withdrawing. Michelle also had difficulty with some expressive language skills (e.g., word retrieval). She rarely volunteered to answer questions in class because of the difficulty she had in quickly finding the words to express ideas and because of difficulty understanding the lessons taught in the large-group classroom setting.

Michelle's teacher brought her concerns regarding Michelle to the school-based team of specialists. This particular teacher accurately believed that Michelle was a motivated youngster but that "something is interfering with her ability to learn." Michelle's parents found that she was able to understand verbal statements at home and was able to communicate thoughts and ideas to them, but Michelle often required repetition of statements if they were in certain restaurants or other somewhat noisy environments.

Michelle received a psychological, an educational, and a speech-language evaluation to identify the specific nature of her strengths and deficits. Results indicated that Michelle was a bright child who had exceptional visual memory skills and whose academic performance was on grade level. This latter fact may have been due to the tutoring she received and early-morning school meetings with her teacher. Speech-language evaluations showed that Michelle had central auditory–processing deficits and word-retrieval weaknesses. An audiologist diagnosed Michelle as having a central auditory–processing disorder.

The team, along with her parents, agreed that Michelle should attend a resource room program (where lessons could be reinforced in a quieter small-group setting) and speech-language therapy. In the classroom, Michelle was seated toward the front of the room. To decrease extraneous noises, the classroom door was kept shut when the teacher gave lessons. Her tests were designed in multiple-choice format to cut down on the impact of word-retrieval difficulties on her performance. The Committee on Special Education supported these recommendations. Michelle responded positively to the interventions and to learning that she had numerous areas of cognitive strength. The interventions also allowed Michelle to understand the lessons more easily, thus leading to her improved view of her own intellectual abilities.

Pragmatic Language and "Body Language" Deficits

What about those children who appear to understand the classroom lessons and can sustain attention when others speak, yet repeatedly misinterpret social cues? For the purpose of this discussion, *pragmatic language skills* refer to one's ability to understand and respond to verbal and nonverbal social language and interactions (e.g., body language, humor).

PETER: SOCIAL CONFUSION

Peter had trouble in this skill area. He was a very serious third grader. He wanted to have friends but was often shunned by his peers. Peter's difficulties seemed to focus on his concrete interpretation of spoken language, his lack of focus on nonverbal cues, and his difficulty responding to the jokes initiated by his peer group. Peter, for instance, became upset when a group of students laughingly told him that "you have to stay in third grade again next year!" Peter was unsure whether this was a joke or not, and he was unsure how to respond. Peter received numerous forms of intervention, including social skills training and speech-language therapy. His teacher also spoke to the class about tolerance. Peter continues to struggle socially, but he is more likely to use all forms of communication—such as verbal, facial, and body language—to help him understand the social cues and situation.

Suggestions for Teachers: Factors to Consider in Assessing Language Deficits

Let us return to our exploration of possible causes of Evan's and Lisa's behavioral symptoms. Both may be suffering from receptive and/or expressive language problems. When a child feels inadequate in his or her ability to understand class work, secondary emotional and behavioral reactions may occur. It is possible that Evan acted out, while Lisa withdrew, because of their awareness that they could not easily follow the teacher's lessons. A speech-language pathologist would need more information regarding their language-based skills before determining whether significant language concerns exist. Once again, children's behaviors may alert us to a problem situation, but it is not always easy to determine the nature of that problem.

At times, it is hard to differentiate a child with central auditory–processing problems from a child with an attention-deficit disorder (ADD), especially when hyperactive symptoms are absent. Both disorders may involve an "inability to sustain attention, seemingly weak figure–ground skills, and difficulty processing (or focusing on) lengthy and complex sentences" (Moss & Sheiffele, 1994, p. 95).

A child who appears to have language deficits may have other areas of difficulty as well. The diagnosis of a language disorder does not rule out the presence of other learning disabilities, emotional issues, medical problems, and so on. In addition, some children can appear to have trouble with language *because* of other factors; for example, a depressed youngster may lack the emotional energy to focus on the teacher's lesson and an ADD child may similarly lack focus on the lesson despite the fact that both students possess the ability to effectively understand and use verbal language.

One advantage of having a school-based, interdisciplinary team of professionals is that the areas of functioning relevant to the particular child's difficulties can be explored if necessary. However, not all children require psychological, educational, and speech-language assessments. Some students may meet only with one professional, who will then make recommendations or implement specific educational modifications. Later, if that professional and the classroom teacher are not satisfied with the student's progress, then the team might review other possibilities regarding further assessment and, perhaps, additional interventions.

There is a risk in not having all professionals test a child because certain unexpected areas of deficit might not be initially uncovered. However, as mentioned previously, classroom teachers should also consider the fact that there are risks to having a child receive many tests because the child may feel scrutinized or become very self-conscious. Sometimes informal assessments, such as a brief interview with the student or an unobtrusive classroom observation, can allow a professional to begin the process of designing an intervention strategy. At other times the professional may conclude, after initial assessments, that the child actually does not appear to be impaired and that no immediate child-focused intervention is needed. For instance, one evaluator learned that a struggling reader's peer group was unusually advanced and reading a particularly challenging book in class. This reader, who appeared to be struggling when compared to his peer group, actually had age-appropriate reading skills with no prior history of reading problems. This student now struggled because he was asked to read a book that was typically assigned to older children. In this situation, the teacher, not the student, needed to adjust the curriculum to meet the needs of the student. The confident, open teacher can accept such comments and adjust the material if it is in the best interest of the students.

CONCLUSION

To conclude this chapter, it is important to restate that a child must be viewed from a holistic perspective so that cognitive, social, emotional, behavioral, and physical issues can be explored, if indicated. This chapter summarized the topics of intelligence, learning disabilities, and language issues. Our case examples, Evan and Lisa, allowed us to see that overt symptoms do not always point to a specific disorder. Therefore, a multidisciplinary approach is recommended for investigating the underlying cause of a symptom. In later chapters, other possible problems that could lead to Evan's and Lisa's symptoms are explored.

REFERENCES

American Psychiatric Association (APA). (2000). *Diagnostic and statistical manual of mental disorders: Fourth edition, DSM-IV-TR, text revision*. Washington, DC: Author.

Crnic, K. A., & Reid, M. (1989). Mental retardation. In E. J. Mash & R. A. Barkley (Eds.), *Treatment of childhood disorders* (pp. 247–285). New York: Guilford.

Feldhusen, J. F., & Moon, S. M. (1992). Grouping gifted students: Issues and concerns. *Gifted Child Quarterly, 36*(2), 63–67.

Gaddes, W. H. (1985). *Learning disabilities and brain function: A neuropsychological approach* (2nd ed.). New York: Springer-Verlag.

Gardner, H. (1999). *Intelligence reframed: Multiple intelligences for the 21st century*. New York: Basic Books.

Goleman, D. (1995). *Emotional intelligence*. New York: Bantam.

Gridley, B. E. (1987). Children and giftedness. In A. Thomas & J. Grimes (Eds.), *Children's needs: Psychological perspectives* (pp. 234–241). Washington, DC: National Association of School Psychologists.

Lahey, M. (1988). *Language disorders and language development*. New York: Macmillan.

Lerner, J. (2000). *Learning disabilities: Theories, diagnosis, and teaching strategies* (8th ed.). Boston: Houghton Mifflin.

Levine, M. (1994). *Educational care: A system for understanding and helping children with learning problems at home and in school*. Cambridge, MA: Educators Publishing Service.

Moss, W. L. (2002). Understanding giftedness. In L. W. Brainerd, *Homeschooling your gifted child: Language arts for the middle school years* (pp. 1–23). New York: LearningExpress.

Moss, W. L., & Sheiffele, W. A. (1994). Can we differentially diagnose an attention deficit disorder without hyperactivity from a central auditory processing problem? *Child Psychiatry and Human Development, 25*(2), 85–96.

Neisser, U., Boodoo, G., Bouchard, T. J., Boykin, A. W., Brody, N., Ceci, S. J., Halpern, D. F., Loehlin, J. C., Perloff, R., Sternberg, R. J., & Urbina, S. (1996). Intelligence: Knowns and unknowns. *American Psychologist, 51*(2), 77–101.

Pennington, B. F. (1991). *Diagnosing learning disorders: A neuropsychological framework*. New York: Guilford.

Rohrer, J. C. (1995). Primary teacher conceptions of giftedness: Image, evidence, and nonevidence. *Journal for the Education of the Gifted, 18*(3), 269–283.

Shaywitz, B. A., Fletcher, J. M., & Shaywitz, S. E. (1995). Defining and classifying learning disabilities and attention-deficit/hyperactivity disorder. *Journal of Child Neurology, 10* (Supplement No. 1), S50–S57.

Sparrow, S. S., & Gurland, S. T. (1998). Assessment of gifted children with the WISC-III. In A. Prifitera & D. H. Saklofske (Eds.), *WISC-III clinical use and interpretation: Scientist-practitioner perspectives* (pp. 59–61). San Diego: Academic Press.

Sternberg, R. J., & Grigorenko, E. L. (2002). Difference scores in the identification of children with learning disabilities: It's time to use a different method. *Journal of School Psychology, 40*(1), 65–83.

Taylor, H. G. (1989). Learning disabilities. In E. J. Mash & R. A. Barkley (Eds.), *Treatment of childhood disorders* (pp. 347–380). New York: Guilford.

CHAPTER 3

Trauma and Stress

*Trauma; Posttraumatic Stress Disorder; World Violence;
Community Violence; Coping with Traumatic Events*

In this and the next chapter, various forms of stress, including trauma, are reviewed. This chapter focuses on trauma and posttraumatic stress disorder and explores ways in which educators can assist students in times of crisis. A review of studies on how individuals have reacted to wars and community violence is also discussed.

Even the youngest students are often aware of the violent events that occur across the nation and the world. When they are exposed to world, community, school, or home stressors, the impact on their emotional availability to learn and to thrive can be dramatic.

CHRIS: DISTRACTED AND DISTANT

Chris's third-grade teacher phoned his mother, Mrs. Patterson, to report that Chris had recently become distracted and distant in class. Mrs. Patterson was able to offer a likely explanation. She commented that Chris had been preoccupied, during the prior month, with television news reports about a student who shot a classmate. Despite the fact that this tragedy had occurred in another state, Chris had become anxious, experienced nightmares, and expressed concern about his personal safety as well as the safety of his classmates and family members.

Mrs. Patterson agreed to allow her son to speak with the school's counselor about his fears. Shortly after learning about the safeguards in place in school and the training that the teachers had recently undergone to learn about techniques that could be used when responding to angry students, Chris became less anxious and more attentive during class. He continued to meet with the counselor to help ameliorate his general fears of violence. Chris's response to the news coverage exemplifies how a situation that does not directly impact a student's community can still have an immense effect on a young life.

DEFINING TRAUMATIC EVENTS

A *traumatic event* can be described as an event that threatens one's physical or psychological welfare (Brewin, Dalgleish, & Joseph, 1996) and can lead to "a disordered psychic or behavioral state" (Garbarino, Kostelny, & Dubrow, 1991, p. 377). Brewin and colleagues (1996) support a definition where "there is no implication that psychological trauma must involve an event outside the ordinary range of human experience, although it may do so" (p. 675).

The individual's interpretation of, and emotional response to, an event may be highly personal and emotionally stressful, even when the specific event may not be viewed as traumatic by others. In other words, not all children who have been exposed to similar stress or identical situations will become traumatized and display debilitating repercussions, even when such reactions do occur for a subgroup of youngsters.

ROBERT, ELIZABETH, AND TOM: TRAUMATIZED?

Robert was a conscientious student who studied hard and sought to please his parents. He knew that they had high hopes for him and expected him to follow in their footsteps by attending an Ivy League college. Therefore, when he returned home from school with a B on a test, he hid the paper from his parents and ultimately suffered severe anxiety and guilt about the test grade and his resultant actions. For many other students, a similar grade would not have led to such emotional turmoil.

Teasing can be quite disturbing to many children, although not all youngsters will be traumatized by it. Elizabeth just smiled when she returned to school after an orthodontist appointment and was teased about her new braces. Tom, however, felt humiliated and horrified when a peer made fun of his new glasses. He complained of stomachaches and tried to avoid going to school for the next few days following the incident. Therefore, it is not always easy to tell which situations might leave a child feeling hurt, uncomfortable, or emotionally traumatized.

POSTTRAUMATIC STRESS DISORDER (PTSD)

Defining PTSD

When a person experiences emotional trauma, with symptoms persisting beyond a period of one month, there is a risk that he or she is suffering from a posttraumatic stress disorder (PTSD). According to the American Psychiatric Association (APA) (2000), PTSD can occur after an individual

> has been exposed to a traumatic event in which both of the following were present: (1) the person experienced, witnessed, or was confronted with an event

or events that involved actual or threatened death or serious injury, or a threat
to the physical integrity of self or others . . . (2) the person's response involved
intense fear, helplessness, or horror . . . [for] children, this may be expressed
instead by disorganized or agitated behavior. (p. 467)

The American Psychiatric Association (2000) also notes that symptoms
create "distress or impairment" (p. 468) in one's ability to function. PTSD
symptoms can include:

recurrent and intrusive distressing recollections . . . [for] young children, repetitive play may occur in which themes or aspects of the trauma are expressed;
. . . recurrent distressing dreams of the event . . . [for] children, there may be
frightening dreams without recognizable content; . . . acting or feeling as if the
traumatic event were recurring . . . [for] young children, trauma-specific reen-
actment may occur; . . . distress at exposure to . . . cues that symbolize or resemble an aspect of the traumatic event; . . . [and] physiological reactivity on
exposure to internal or external cues that symbolize or resemble the traumatic
event. (APA, 2000, p. 468)

It has also been reported that those suffering from PTSD may display a
range of reactions, including withdrawal of energy from relationships, from
formerly pleasurable activities, and/or from reflections about the trauma;
sleep changes; mood changes (e.g., "irritability"); attentional struggles, and
"hypervigilance" (APA, 2000, p. 468).

Anthony, Lonigan, and Hecht (1999) comment that PTSD "manifests
in three symptom clusters, Intrusion/Active Avoidance, Numbing/Passive
Avoidance, and Arousal" (p. 335). The authors investigated the effects
of a hurricane on young people aged 9 to 19. They noted that symptoms of
posttraumatic stress were similar for children from late childhood through
late adolescence, although the symptoms were found to be more severe
in younger children. Anthony and colleagues (1999) propose that symptoms, such as a loss of interest in that which had brought pleasure, "attention problems, and learning/memory problems[,] . . . may be more
appropriately considered associated, rather than diagnostic, features of
PTSD" (p. 334).

Brewin and colleagues (1996) report that PTSD is characterized by intrusive, recurrent memories that can be associated with a specific traumatic
event and that the "trauma can be so overwhelming that processing may
be involuntarily suspended and the individual may experience emotional
numbing" (p. 678). Some PTSD sufferers, according to these authors, "may
attempt to deliberately interfere with this processing by distracting themselves
and systematically avoiding either reminders of the trauma in general or
reminders of specific aspects of the trauma" (p. 678).

LESLIE AND ZACHARY: DIAGNOSED WITH PTSD

I have had the opportunity to speak with numerous children suffering from trauma and/or PTSD symptoms. For instance, 11-year-old Leslie witnessed her neighbor being stabbed and robbed. She subsequently experienced frequent violent nightmares of people suddenly being attacked. In her waking state, she experienced a loss of pleasure, had flashbacks of the event, and was hypervigilant as she suspiciously glanced around her environment, expecting danger. Because of generalized anxiety about her own safety, she displayed a lack of interest and effort in her academic work. Her teacher reported that these symptoms did not predate the time when Leslie witnessed the stabbing and did not seem to be decreasing in the months following the trauma. This young student met the diagnostic criteria for having PTSD, despite the fact that she objectively realized that the perpetrators were behind bars and could not harm her.

Months after the terrorist act of September 11, 2001, Zachary displayed symptoms of distress in his fifth-grade classroom, including agitation, irritability, and inattention. His father noted that Zachary had become very concerned about his parents' whereabouts and cried easily when he spoke of the losses that families across the country had experienced on that day. Zachary had frequent memories of that event and suffered from sleep difficulties as well as from separation anxiety. On further inquiry, it was found that Zachary met the criteria for PTSD.

LISA AND EVAN: COULD THEY HAVE PTSD?

If we return to our two case examples from Chapter 1, Lisa and Evan, we can explore whether they might be suffering from PTSD. Lisa's second-grade teacher described her as sad and commented that Lisa did not typically interact with peers or smile. Lisa was also noted to have difficulty completing her classwork. Could Lisa have PTSD? It would be important to identify a traumatic event that occurred prior to the emergence of her symptoms. On the surface, it would seem easy to determine whether Lisa had been exposed to a terrifying experience. Wouldn't her parents or her teacher know about it? Unfortunately, this is not always the case. At times, children seek to ignore or *forget* a painful incident, or they may attempt to protect the adults by not reporting upsetting events. Physical, sexual, or emotional abuse may be particularly difficult for youngsters to report, since they may seek to protect the perpetrators, may feel personal shame, or may blame themselves for the abuse.

A thorough clinical interview may be indicated if Lisa's parents or teacher suspect PTSD. In preparation for such a diagnostic assessment, the teacher (and parents) might be able to provide the interviewer with pertinent information regarding Lisa's emotional and behavioral state, any recent changes in either her emotions or behaviors, recent stressors, as well as information on her social relationships, school life, and family. The evaluator may recommend formal testing to rule out potential alternative explanations for her symptoms (e.g., depression, learning disability, low energy due to physical ailments) and to more closely explore her cognitive profile and emotional concerns.

Evan, the other child who was initially presented in Chapter 1, presents very differently. He is a sixth grader who has challenged his teacher, does not complete his assignments, and frequently leaves the room to go to the bathroom or to get a drink of water. Unfortunately, there is no one way that children can communicate the cause of their actions. Youngsters may become irritable or agitated as a reaction to a trauma. Evan displayed overt symptoms of both irritability and agitation. Once again, however, it would be important to determine whether there was a triggering event that elicited the symptoms. The event may not be one that objectively put him in danger, but he may have perceived the situation as presenting a threat. For instance, the World Trade Center attack in New York City on September 11, 2001, may have led Evan to believe that he could be the next victim.

Research on the Effects of War and Violence

It is important for teachers to become aware of which children are more vulnerable during traumatic times and what factors may protect them from developing PTSD. Educators are in a unique position to interact with many youngsters, to assist them daily with many of their academic and emotional needs, and to identify those who may need help to cope with their response to stressful events. Before discussing how to assist specific students today, it is useful to turn to the research literature to learn about the findings that have emerged from the study of survivors of wartime conflicts and about the effects on children of exposure to violence.

Holocaust Survivors. Research on Holocaust survivors has allowed investigators to increase their knowledge about the long-term effects of severe, persistent stress and traumatization (Shmotkin & Lomranz, 1998). Following World War II, many "professionals" apparently believed that death camp survivors of the Holocaust "had lost all chances for a normal or even a tolerable life" (Suedfeld, 2000, p. 5).

Despite these dire predictions, Suedfeld (2000) reports that some of the survivors who had been in "the group of irretrievably damaged Buchenwald Children" became "outstanding citizens," such as "Robert Waisman, a respected businessman and philanthropist in Vancouver, Meir Lau, the Ashkenazi Chief Rabbi of Israel, and Nobel laureate Elie Wiesel" (p. 5). This information is crucial for educators to keep in mind, since it indicates that there is a chance for even those exposed to extreme trauma to thrive in their futures. However, while Suedfeld did find that Holocaust survivors' general "attitudes about the world" were similar to those found in a "comparison group" and that they had "a higher sense of self-worth (survivor pride)," the "survivors tend to trust others less" and "ascribe people's outcomes more to luck and chance than to personal control" (p. 6).

Shmotkin and Lomranz (1998) note that Holocaust survivors are not a homogeneous group but rather fall into subgroups. For instance, they state that those survivors in their study who seemed to be more vocal about their traumatic Holocaust experiences appear to feel "remarkably positive about themselves," while others "still bear the psychological scars privately while leading a normal, though less happy, life" (p. 150).

These findings seem to suggest that talking about difficult experiences may have a beneficial effect. In fact, many therapists have postulated this very view and have developed support groups (e.g., bereavement groups, cancer support groups, groups for parents and children experiencing divorce) to help children and adults cope with numerous areas of stress.

BRIAN: HELPED BY TALKING WITH OTHERS

Ten-year-old Brian, for instance, had been having difficulty concentrating in school and withdrew from his friends during the period immediately following his parents' separation and divorce. Brian's mother and father both noted this dramatic change and spoke with Brian's classroom teacher. Eventually, it was decided that Brian would be a candidate for the school counselor's group for children of divorce. Brian reluctantly attended the first meeting but then expressed relief to his mother that "the kids in the group know what it's like to get divorced. I don't feel so weird."

Over the next few weeks, Brian began to accept invitations to spend time with his friends again and his teacher reported improvements in his attention to work in class. Many children who are struggling with such issues as divorce can benefit from speaking about their experiences. Some cautions about certain kinds of group or individual coping strategies will be presented shortly (e.g., problem solving directed at trying to find ways to change a situation that the person is not going to be able to change rather than emotional-coping strategies to deal with the stress).

Vietnam War Research Study. Research on survivors from a variety of wars can provide insights into the effects of stressful experiences on individuals and on groups. For example, in a study of male Vietnam veterans who served in the Army, Barrett and colleagues (1996) found that there was a significant increase in antisocial behavior in those men who met the criteria for PTSD. The authors theorize that the symptoms of PTSD, "such as numbing of affect, disruptive intrusive symptoms, and hypervigilance" (p. 580), may have made these individuals more vulnerable to difficulties in personal and work relationships.

In school, a child suffering from PTSD may also have difficulties with social and academic functioning, even when there is no display of antisocial behavior.

FRANK: HYPERVIGILANCE

Frank's postwar difficulties can highlight the impact that PTSD can have on one's life. Twenty years after he returned from service in the Vietnam War, Frank continued to show PTSD symptoms. He admitted that he hated going to movie theaters because he would be unable to observe his surroundings and predict the action of others. When he was in a room with other people, Frank positioned himself in the corner of the room so that "no one can sneak up behind me." Although he did not engage in antisocial behaviors, his flashbacks of his war experience, hypervigilance, and mistrust of others significantly impacted his ability to find employment and rewarding social relationships. Frank's experience lends support to the idea that PTSD symptoms can be long term and subjectively painful. Therefore, it is important that teachers be aware of the symptoms and seek appropriate assistance for those struggling with the emotional repercussions.

Gulf War Research. Klingman (1992) specifically studied the effects of war on students. He assessed students' responses to the missile attacks on Israel during the Gulf War. Results suggested that there was a "reduction in the incidence of stress reaction during the first 4 weeks of the war" and that it "may be attributed to either verbal denial . . . or to the habituation phenomenon" (pp. 524–525). Habituation refers to the decrease of sensitivity or reactivity to a situation or to a stimulus. However, not all individuals will deny or habituate after being exposed to war. In fact, Klingman noted that some youngsters might actually have the opposite response and display increased sensitivity.

Weisenberg, Schwarzwald, Waysman, Solomon, and Klingman (1993) also studied student responses to the Gulf War. They collected data on 492 Israeli children several weeks after the end of the war. Results suggested that those who dealt with the threat by trying to implement problem-solving techniques rather than by using "avoidance and distraction" showed an increase in postwar emotional distress (p. 466). The authors explain that the results "indicate that there are times when avoidance is highly effective: persisting in problem-focused coping in a situation that cannot be changed can lead to undesirable consequences" (p. 466). In regard to young children, the authors speculate that they may have had more difficulty than older youngsters in emotionally denying the "external threats" (p. 466) and therefore had more difficulty coping with the stressful events.

There appear to be times when debriefing (i.e., discussing traumatic events), finding adaptive ways to focus energy (i.e., starting a campaign against a disease after a loved one dies from the illness), and distraction may all be beneficial for some individuals at particular times. Weisenberg and colleagues' (1993) findings suggest, however, that there are situations when a child may encounter frustration and further stress if problem-solving strategies are employed and judged to be ineffective.

Coping After September 11, 2001. Following the events of September 11, 2001, I had the opportunity to interact with many parents, educators, and children of elementary school age. While some children appeared to avoid thinking about the events and became upset when others brought up the topic, other children asked many questions and wanted to watch the television news coverage. As Weisenberg and colleagues (1993) found in their study, I observed that the children who wanted to problem-solve to make sure the terrorist acts would never occur again often became angry at, and nervous about, their inability to assure their own safety. At times, this anger was also directed toward parents, who children typically believe have the responsibility of protecting them.

War in the Sarajevo Region. Zvizdic and Butollo (2000) studied adolescents who were between the ages of 6 and 12 at the time of the 1992–1995 war in the Sarajevo region. Their findings suggest that "extensive exposure to war and postwar stressful/traumatic events is significantly related to the level of depressive reactions in early adolescents" (p. 213). Depression can also develop in many non-war situations in which children feel helpless or hopeless about their abilities or the situations that they encounter. Twelve-year-old Leroy, for instance, verbalized symptoms of anhedonia, sadness, and hopelessness, and noted that he was "stupid," because he felt incapable of coping with the street violence he witnessed. Here again, the connection between war experiences and exposure to other traumas is evident.

Other Research on the Effects of War. Layne and colleauges (2001) reviewed some of the literature on children living in areas of war and note that post-traumatic stress disorder can be an associated reaction to severe environmental stressors, such as being exposed to war. These authors state that these high-stress situations may lead to "depression, complicated grief reactions, academic difficulties, somatic complaints, disturbances in family and peer relationships, substance abuse, and a variety of other adverse outcomes" (p. 278). However, in their own study of students residing in Bosnia and Herzegovina, the authors found that intervention can help ameliorate some of the symptomatology. Intervention strategies will be described later in this chapter.

DAVID: THE IMPACT OF WITNESSING VIOLENCE

Many of the symptoms described by Layne and colleagues (2001) were found in 16-year-old David. David witnessed the murder of his mother, the daily gang wars in his neighborhood, and the change from living with his mother to living in foster care. He displayed symptoms of PTSD. He began using drugs to dull his pain, and he was angry most of the time. David admitted that he perceived academic work as "a waste. I'll be dead soon anyway." He denied suicidal intent but felt helpless to protect himself from others. David eventually began "doing what I wanted. I robbed, I did drugs, I cut school, and I just hung out." Despite this "doing what I want" lifestyle, David admitted to being unhappy. Eventually, a supportive neighbor helped David understand that he still had some power for making decisions in his life and that he could make better choices than the ones he was selecting. For David, the story has taken a positive turn. He enrolled in an alternative educational program and now resides in a group home in a neighborhood where he feels safer.

Who Might Be More Vulnerable to Trauma?

After September 11, 2001, children, parents, and teachers scrambled to comprehend the magnitude of the events and how these events might impact the rest of their lives. DeAngelis (2002b) stated that work conducted by Dr. Annette La Greca, regarding children who were significantly affected by Hurricane Andrew, was useful in identifying the potentially most vulnerable children in natural and unnatural tragedies (e.g., 9/11). DeAngelis notes that La Greca's research found that youngsters who may be at greater risk of later emotional difficulties include those who had believed that their lives were in more acute danger, those with fewer stable supports from significant people in their lives, and those whose day-to-day lives were more affected by a highly disruptive life situation. In addition, the author reports that maladaptive coping strategies, "such as blaming oneself and others" (p. 31) as well as premorbid adjustment difficulties and/or anxiety symptoms, may leave a child more vulnerable to symptoms of posttraumatic stress disorder following exposure to a traumatic event.

Although it may be difficult, if not impossible, for each individual to find a way to stop a hurricane, terrorist attack, or war, there is much that teachers can do to help students to be better equipped to cope with disasters and to help them to minimize the emotional damage that might occur following a war or trauma. At the conclusion of this chapter, possible steps that teachers can take to assist students are explored. First, however, it is important to review some of the violent situations that may occur in a child's own community and might lead to traumatic reactions.

VIOLENCE IN THE CHILD'S COMMUNITY

While school-based violence has received much media coverage in the last few years, Evans and Rey (2001) report that "school homicide represents a low frequency but high impact expression of violence" (p. 157). School violence is addressed in the context of bullying in Chapters 4 and 6, and in the context of aggressive youth in Chapter 6. In this section, the powerful effects of living in a neighborhood impacted by community violence is explored.

Mascolo (1998) notes that violence in urban communities is so prevalent that it "has reached epidemic proportions" (p. 37). There are large numbers of youth who are victimized (Kliewer, Lepore, Oskin, & Johnson, 1998; Schwartz & Proctor, 2000). Therefore, community violence and its impact on youngsters warrants further exploration in this section.

In a study of fourth, fifth, and sixth graders from 14 different classrooms in two elementary schools, Schwartz and Proctor (2000) found that there are numerous potential consequences that can occur after being exposed to violence in one's own community. For instance, they note that such exposure can be correlated with social, emotional, and behavioral difficulties and concerns. Since school is not an encapsulated experience that is completely sheltered or protected from the outside world, these symptoms and reactions (e.g., PTSD, anxiety, depression, and other negative effects) of exposure to violence are likely to be evident in the academic setting.

Mascolo (1998) reviewed the literature and found similar data to that presented by Schwartz and Proctor regarding the possible aftereffects of a youngster's exposure to violence. Mascolo also reports that, in some students, academic performance may be negatively affected when the child experiences violent life events. He further states that there is a positive correlation between the level of anxiety that a child feels from experiencing violence and the level of subsequent behavioral problems exhibited. In my professional experience, I have found that the behavioral problems in the young child may be exhibited in many different ways, such as by withdrawal and apathy or by more overt, acting-out behaviors.

Mascolo (1998) adds that educators may be able to detect symptoms and that it is important to understand the cause, since children exposed to community violence may display behaviors that can be misidentified and lead to a child "being labeled incorrectly as inattentive, unmotivated, or lacking in ability" (p. 52).

Although not all children suffer from debilitating symptoms or PTSD after exposure to violence (Osofsky, 1995), many negative effects can occur. Saltzman and colleagues (2001) reviewed literature on adolescents who had been exposed to violent situations. They note that some of the difficulties that can emerge after such an experience can "include reduced academic achievement; aggressive, delinquent, or high-risk sexual behaviors; and substance abuse and dependence" (p. 291). They add that trauma has also been associated with "long-term developmental disturbances, including disrupted moral development, missed developmental opportunities, delayed preparation for professional and family life, and disruptions in close relationships" in adolescents (p. 291).

Garbarino and colleauges (1991) report that some children, after being exposed to violence, can develop adaptive strategies for coping with the realistically dangerous situation but then generalize these strategies toward other situations where the coping strategies are no longer adaptive or appropriate. These authors comment that aggressive actions, for example, may be protective in some instances for youngsters exposed to persistent violence yet maladaptive when brought into a school situation where the violence may be subjectively feared but objectively nonexistent.

On a positive note, Garbarino and colleagues (1991) state that parental influence can diminish the child's maladaptive coping patterns as long as the parents are not emotionally overwhelmed themselves. If this occurs, then these authors comment that "the development of young children deteriorates rapidly and markedly" (p. 380).

JOHN AND RICHARD: TRYING TO COPE

Thirteen-year-old John and his family display how exposure to street violence and varying levels of emotional nurturance and support can impact a child's behavior and emotional functioning. John, his mother, and his six siblings all lived on the street in a high-crime section of a large city. John's mother was often emotionally unavailable and physically ill due to her daily use of drugs. John (the oldest child) and Richard (the second oldest) both displayed behaviors that were generally useful on the street but counterproductive in school. For instance, they became immediately suspicious when someone looked at them, they had an expectation that others would harm them, and they were typically agitated and easily angered. John and Richard stopped attending school when they were 10 and 9, respectively, because of the discomfort of having to listen to their teacher, concentrate on academic work, share materials, and handle the challenges of peer pressure and peer interactions. In addition, the frequent wanderings of the family made attendance in one school an almost impossible task. While they did not use drugs, they frequently stole food and robbed people for money. These latter two behaviors, according to John, were important for survival.

John and Richard did not have a parent who displayed the ability to cope with life's stressors; this would put them at higher risk for difficulty, according to Garbarino and colleagues (1991). Each of these boys displayed struggles in coping with school and peer relationships. Interestingly, however, their four younger siblings did not show the same severity of symptoms. They were more trusting, were less angry, and displayed less agitation and emotional lability. Upon inquiry, it became evident that John and Richard had taken on the parental caregiver role with the younger children, listening to them, supporting them, giving them food, and giving them a sense of stability. It is possible that the younger siblings displayed fewer symptoms partially because of the parenting they received from their older brothers.

In sum, since children show traumatic reactions in various ways and in ways that may mimic other difficulties (e.g., depression, a conduct disorder, anxiety), it can be difficult for an educator to immediately know the root of the behavior unless all the information is available. Therefore, teachers should be alert to the symptoms and consider the possibility that a student has been exposed to violence. If an educator is aware that a student, or the entire student population, has experienced a traumatic situation, what can be done? Let's explore this question.

Suggestions for Teachers: Responding to Violence, Devastating News, or a Disaster

There are many possible crisis scenarios that would create the need for a teacher and school community to implement an emergency response plan. The response may vary, depending on the age of the students, the philosophy of the administration, the policies of the school board, and the nature of the crisis (e.g., death of a beloved faculty member; death of a child's parent; gun-wielding intruder into the school building; tornado; terrorist attack). However, there are some general suggestions that an educator might consider when contemplating a response to devastating news.

Hobfoll and colleagues (1991) comment that "children's reactions will often mirror the reactions of their parents" (p. 853). As children turn to parents to see their reactions to new situations and crises, youngsters also will turn to teachers. If their caregiver is emotionally overwhelmed, children may become quite upset and may even worry about who is available to keep them safe.

Take Time to Gain Composure—When Possible. Since students can be impacted by the emotional state of the adults around them, it might be beneficial if educators take a few minutes after learning about a crisis event (if feasible) to reflect on personal reactions to the trauma and to assess whether the task of focusing on the needs of the children is realistic.

MRS. KRAMER: TIME TO PROCESS THE EVENT

Mrs. Kramer arrived at school at 8:00 A.M. on Monday morning and learned that the elementary school's music teacher (age 43) had died of a heart attack over the weekend. Mrs. Kramer immediately became tearful and needed to sit down because she felt physically ill from the news. When it was time to begin the schoolday, the principal asked Mrs. Kramer if she felt able to teach. Mrs. Kramer, realizing that she needed time to pull herself together, asked the principal if someone could briefly cover her class. The principal luckily had the ability to arrange coverage for a half-hour.

Mrs. Kramer sat quietly, reflecting on her fondness for the deceased, on the shock of the news, and also on her personal panic that set in when she heard the news and realized that she would soon be the same age as her stricken colleague. Later, when she entered the classroom, she was able to provide the focus and attitude that conveyed safety for the children, who would later learn of the loss.

Who Breaks the News? If a disaster occurs during the schoolday, the administration must determine whether the parents will be the ones who will decide how and when to communicate the news to the youngsters or whether the students must be told while they are in the school building. Sometimes this decision is quite clear. If a hurricane is threatening the integrity of the school building, the administration must immediately safeguard the children and, perhaps, move them to another location. However, if a war breaks out in another country, there is more time to communicate with parents about their wishes. After the terrorist attacks of September 11, 2001, some schools had time to contact parents (e.g., a school far from the attacks), while others did not (e.g., schools within the immediate vicinity of the World Trade Center in New York).

Explaining the Situation. If educators must be the ones to tell the students about world/community tragedies, the information should be stated in a way that leaves the door open to allowing parents to later explain the events in a way that fits with their religious, cultural, and philosophical views. As the school community tries to cope with a specific stress, regular parent–teacher contact can help develop a unified approach to helping the children, a way for parents to learn about the school's intervention plan, and a way for educators to learn about parental concerns as well as parental perceptions of how their children are reacting.

Helping Children to Cope with Stress. If children are aware of the traumatic situation, what can a teacher do to help them through the stress? First of all, all individuals (young children, adolescents, and adults) have "basic needs" related to "hunger, nurturance, and security" (Chatters, 1987, p. 212). When planning ways to help students cope with trauma, it would be helpful to keep these three priorities in mind.

Nurturance. Nurturance, or reassurance, has been cited in the literature as an important component of any response plan designed to assist children (e.g., DeAngelis, 2002a; Garbarino et al., 1991; Hobfoll et al., 1991). Reassurance may take many forms, including letting youngsters know that they can take you, their teacher, on the side and speak about feelings and concerns. This allows a student to have some privacy when discussing feelings, and it also prevents the potential of the contagion of fear—one child speaks of fear and then another child panics from hearing about the peer's anxiety. Hobfoll and colleagues (1991) suggest that adults should protect children from the personal anxieties of the adults, listen to their concerns in a supportive manner without being judgmental, and offer them comfort and "reassurance" (p. 853).

Support in a structured, familiar environment. Research shows that children appear to benefit from feelings of support, whether the traumatic stress is acute (e.g., Garbarino et al., 1991) or chronic (Kliewer et al., 1998). Masten and Coatsworth (1998) note that studies have shown that youngsters "at risk" benefit from a combination of "warm, structured child rearing" and "reasonably high expectations" (p. 215). Although this research focused on parental roles, teachers can certainly adopt this information into their role in the classroom. In fact, keeping students in a supportive, familiar, structured routine sometimes will give them a feeling of security. School routines are typically well established, and maintenance of this structure, as appropriate, conveys a feeling that a child's entire world has not been shattered (e.g., DeAngelis, 2002a).

Reassuring comments that are not misleading. Offering students reassuring comments to help them feel safe during times of crisis can be quite important, provided that the statements are not misleading. For instance, following the terrorist acts of September 11, 2001, a caring adult may have thought to tell a child that "You will be OK. The terrorists only attack important places." However, this statement could mean that school, which is generally an important place in the eyes of children, could be attacked. It could also lead to fears of going to historical sites in the future. Letting students know that there are safety precautions in place to minimize their risk and that *you*, their teacher, feel safe (if this is truthful) can help them to relax a bit.

Positive use of energy. At a time when disaster occupies everyone's thoughts, it may not be possible to shift the focus to the positive. However, when appropriate, turning the negative into a focus on the positive could help children to feel more competent in their world. For instance, after a hurricane, some older children may want to consider how they can help their community. The act of helping may create a "sense of mastery and control" in the helpers (Hobfoll et al., 1991, p. 853).

After a violent episode in the local community, some youngsters may want to work on a project about the best ways for problem resolution or ways to increase community safety. As noted earlier, however, focusing specifically on the trauma may overwhelm some students who need protection from the intense focus that is sometimes given to a crisis event. One young child explained that his parents were continually watching a television news program that extensively covered wartime battles. This insightful student commented that he should not have watched the news coverage, because "it got me very sad." Chatters (1987) and DeAngelis (2002a) caution adults to monitor a child's exposure to media coverage of stressful situations.

Classroom discussions. Classroom discussions about the trauma and about students' feelings should be carefully considered, with the pros and cons weighed. Classroom discussions can vary greatly, depending on the age of the students, the nature of the trauma, and so on. At times, these group discussions can allow children to sense that they are not alone in their feelings and they can learn more about the current event. However, at other times, a student may become distressed by the discussion or lesson.

Watch for signs of distress. As a class of students or an individual child tries to cope with trauma, it is important for the educators (along with the parents) to keep a watchful eye for signs of significant distress. Those students who generally display a high level of fear are more likely to develop PTSD (DeAngelis, 2002b) and "maladaptive behaviors" (Mascolo, 1998, p. 52). Young children may communicate distress verbally, behaviorally, or through play. They may also try to adaptively cope with their feelings in similar ways.

EXAMPLES OF MALADAPTIVE RESPONSES

- The child who continually verbally berates him- or herself for inadequacies following the trauma (e.g., "I can't do anything right")
- The student who displays increases in physical aggression (e.g., pushing or fighting during basketball games)
- The youngster who perseverates by drawing pictures of the traumatic situation and appears fixated on completing each drawing even when other work is required

JOE: SELF-BLAME

Nine-year-old Joe struggled to cope with the aftereffects of a tornado that destroyed his home. Joe suddenly became extremely conscientious about his work and displayed perfectionistic desires. This was a radical change of behavior from his prior ways of responding to school expectations. Although his newfound focus on school assignments could be interpreted as a positive coping strategy (and may be adaptive for some students), this was not the case for Joe. This youngster personalized the traumatic event and engaged in self-blame. The perfectionism was a form of penance for being "bad" and having been punished by the destruction of his family's house.

EXAMPLES OF MORE ADAPTIVE RESPONSES

- A child initially playing out the disaster but then focusing the play on the rescue workers, the heroes, or the rebuilding of a community
- A child who seeks to make a contribution to a relief fund and then feels a sense of competence because of this action
- A child who openly discusses feelings and then displays increased functioning in daily tasks
- A child who puts more energy into schoolwork because of a desire to take control of life and strive toward success after experiencing out-of-control feelings during a traumatic event

Professional Intervention

Research has suggested that speaking about a trauma can be positive (e.g., Chatters, 1987; Shmotkin & Lomranz, 1998). Saltzman and colleagues (2001) report that "trauma treatment . . . may reduce symptoms of distress and enable students to perform better at school" (p. 301).

Following a stressful situation, teachers are in a position to notice any new social, emotional, or behavioral patterns that children may display. These observations might be helpful to communicate to parents in a nonjudgmental manner. In addition, the school administrators generally have teams of specialists (including mental health staff) available to discuss teacher concerns regarding students. If a teacher feels that a child is suffering distress, the team of specialists may be able to offer an intervention plan that the teacher could implement in the classroom or they may recommend other forms of assistance, such as counseling. Educators are often alone in the classroom but should never be left to feel that they are without a support team.

Reaching Out to the Community

Since some students live in neighborhoods that expose them to significant community violence, teachers and administrators may want to brainstorm ways to reach out to community groups (e.g., police, local organizations) to determine whether any organized collaboration between the school and community can decrease the stress that the students experience.

CONCLUSION

In this chapter, some events that can occur outside the classroom but can greatly affect a student in the classroom have been reviewed. The definition of *trauma*, the symptoms of posttraumatic stress disorder (PTSD), the effects of war, the impact of community violence, and some tools to assist teachers in responding to significant traumas were explored. In addition, a brief discussion about the difficulty in interpreting a student's behavior was revisited. For instance, a review of the fact that both Lisa and Evan could be suffering from PTSD was presented. Lisa and Evan may have suffered trauma and not communicated this to adults, making the PTSD diagnosis more difficult.

There may also be alternative explanations for a child's PTSD symptoms (e.g., depression, anxiety, medical issues, frustration with the struggle of trying to cope with a learning disability), especially if symptoms can be investigated and found to predate the stressful event. Careful assessment of the factors that impact a student is essential in determining an accurate diagnosis and intervention plan.

REFERENCES

American Psychiatric Association (APA). (2000). *Diagnostic and statistical manual of mental disorders: Fourth edition, DSM-IV-TR, text revision*. Washington, DC: Author.

Anthony, J. L., Lonigan, C. J., & Hecht, S. A. (1999). Dimensionality of posttraumatic stress disorder symptoms in children exposed to disaster: Results from confirmatory factor analyses. *Journal of Abnormal Psychology, 108*(2), 326–336.

Barrett, D. H., Resnick, H. S., Foy, D. W., Dansky, B. S., Flanders, W. D., & Stroup, N. E. (1996). Combat exposure and adult psychosocial adjustment among U.S. Army veterans serving in Vietnam, 1965–1971. *Journal of Abnormal Psychology, 105*(4), 575–581.

Brewin, C. R., Dalgleish, T., & Joseph, S. (1996). A dual representation theory of posttraumatic stress disorder. *Psychological Review, 103*(4), 670–686.

Chatters, L. B. (1987). Children and fear of nuclear threat. In A. Thomas & J. Grimes (Eds.), *Children's needs: Psychological perspectives* (pp. 209–214). Washington, DC: National Association of School Psychologists.

DeAngelis, T. (2002a). Helping kids cope with a new threat. *Monitor on psychology: A publication of the American Psychological Association, 33*(4), 33.

DeAngelis, T. (2002b). New lessons on children and stress. *Monitor on psychology: A publication of the American Psychological Association, 33*(4), 30–32.

Evans, G. D., & Rey, J. (2001). In the echoes of gunfire: Practicing psychologists' responses to school violence. *Professional Psychology: Research and Practice, 32*(2), 157–164.

Garbarino, J., Kostelny, K., & Dubrow, N. (1991). What children can tell us about living in danger. *American Psychologist, 46*(4), 376–383.

Hobfoll, S. E., Spielberger, C. D., Breznitz, S., Figley, C., Folkman, S., Lepper-Green, B., Meichenbaum, D., Milgram, N. A., Sandler, I., Sarason, I., & van der Kolk, B. (1991). War-related stress: Addressing the stress of war and other traumatic events. *American Psychologist, 46*(8), 848–855.

Kliewer, W., Lepore, S. J., Oskin, D., & Johnson, P. D. (1998). The role of social and cognitive processes in children's adjustment to community violence. *Journal of Consulting and Clinical Psychology, 66*(1), 199–209.

Klingman, A. (1992). Stress reactions of Israeli youth during the Gulf War: A quantitative study. *Professional Psychology: Research and Practice, 23*(6), 521–527.

Layne, C. M., Pynoos, R. S., Saltzman, W. R., Arslanagic, B., Black, M., Savjak, N., Popovic, T., Durakovic, E., Music, M., Campara, N., Djapo, N., & Houston, R. (2001). Trauma/grief-focused group psychotherapy: School-based postwar intervention with traumatized Bosnian adolescents. *Group Dynamics: Theory, Research, and Practice, 5*(4), 277–290.

Mascolo, J. (1998). Acknowledging, understanding, and assessing the impact of children's exposure to community violence. *The School Psychologist, 52*(2), 37, 47, 52–53, 63, 72.

Masten, A. S., & Coatsworth, J. D. (1998). The development of competence in favorable and unfavorable environments: Lessons from research on successful children. *American Psychologist, 53*(2), 205–220.

Osofsky, J. D. (1995). The effects of exposure to violence on young children. *American Psychologist, 50*(9), 782–788.

Saltzman, W. R., Pynoos, R. S., Steinberg, A. M., Eugene Aisenberg Trauma Psychiatry Service Department of Psychiatry, & Layne, C. M. (2001). Trauma- and grief-focused intervention for adolescents exposed to community violence: Results of a school-based screening and group treatment protocol. *Group Dynamics: Theory, Research, and Practice, 5*(4), 291–303.

Schwartz, D., & Proctor, L. J. (2000). Community violence exposure and children's social adjustment in the school peer group: The mediating roles of emotion regulation and social cognition. *Journal of Consulting and Clinical Psychology, 68*(4), 670–683.

Shmotkin, D., & Lomranz, J. (1998). Subjective well-being among Holocaust survivors: An examination of overlooked differentiations. *Journal of Personality and Social Psychology, 75*(1), 141–155.

Suedfeld, P. (2000). Reverberations of the Holocaust fifty years later: Psychology's contribution to understanding persecution and genocide. *Canadian Psychology, 41*(1), 1–9.

Weisenberg, M., Schwarzwald, J., Waysman, M., Solomon, Z., & Klingman, A. (1993). Coping of school-age children in the sealed room during SCUD missile bombardment and postwar stress reactions. *Journal of Consulting and Clinical Psychology, 61*(3), 462–467.

Zvizdic, S., & Butollo, W. (2000). War-related loss of one's father and persistent depressive reactions in early adolescents. *European Psychologist, 5*(3), 204–214.

CHAPTER 4

Family and School Stress and the Impact of Anxiety

Family Stressors; Victims of Bullying; Anxiety Disorders

In the previous chapter, the potential impact of world and community violence on students was reviewed. This chapter begins with an exploration of how some youngsters may be affected by stressful situations that occur in the child's own home and school. Later in this chapter, anxiety and anxiety disorders are defined and discussed.

STRESS IN THE HOME: BIRTHS, MALTREATMENT, DIVORCE

When a child experiences stress in the home environment, he or she may react with emotional, social, behavioral, or even academic and physiological symptoms (e.g., appetite changes, sleep disturbance, headaches). Stress in the home can develop due to a variety of factors, including maltreatment, parental divorce, remarriage by one or both parents, death, relocation, the birth of a child, and so forth. Any change, even if it is positive, has the potential to create stress.

TIM: POSITIVE EVENT CREATES STRESS

A positive event, such as the birth of a sibling, can create tension for a child. For instance, 9-year-old Tim smiled as he announced to his teacher that his mother had given birth to his sister the previous evening. Later in the week, Tim showed pictures of his sister to his classmates and described how "cute" she was and how he "got to hold her." However, 2 weeks later, after realizing that his sister was not capable of interactive play and that she frequently occupied his mother's attention, Tim was overheard saying, "I wish she'd just go away. I'm sick of her." Tim's teacher noticed that Tim was becoming more irritable and less attentive to lessons. Tim's sister affected his daily routine, his relationship with his parents, and his sleep pattern (his sister kept him up at night because of her crying).

Tim had developmentally intact social skills and eventually found ways to play positively with his newborn sister. Several months after the birth, Tim was more rested, his parents had settled into a routine in which Tim received the attention he desired, and they all appeared to have made a healthy adjustment to the family change. However, Tim and his parents acknowledged that the birth created a period of challenge for them.

Some children appear to adapt more easily than others to the birth of a sibling. Kramer and Gottman (1992) studied a group of children, between 3 and 5 years of age, at a time when they were about to have their first experience with a sibling joining the family unit. These authors found that several factors correlated with more positive sibling relationships, such as "more positive play interactions, fewer unmanaged conflicts, and greater joint participation in extended fantasy play within the peer relationship" (p. 695).

In the next two sections, two forms of stress in the home—maltreatment and divorce—are explored.

The Effects of Child Maltreatment

For the purpose of this discussion, the term *maltreatment* can include references to physical and sexual abuse, neglect, and the witnessing of familial aggression. The potential effects of these traumatic experiences on children have been discussed in many education classes. Teachers have met with me to verbalize their wish to be able to identify and assist abused and neglected children. Unfortunately, there is no one sign that a student will display to indicate maltreatment. In fact, Kendall-Tackett, Williams, and Finkelhor (1993) reviewed some of the literature in the field and note that not all sexually abused children, for instance, display clearly measured symptoms.

Abuse and Neglect. Students who have experienced or are currently experiencing abuse or neglect may display no obvious symptoms or may display signs in a variety of ways, from internalized issues (e.g., anxiety, depression, withdrawal) to externalized difficulties (e.g., aggression, agitation).

ALEX: ADHD? TRAUMATIZED?

Thirteen-year-old Alex was often restless and agitated. His teacher initially consulted the school-based team of specialists because of concerns that Alex might have an attention-deficit hyperactivity disorder (ADHD), that he was not living up to his academic potential, and that he appeared to be "sad." The specialists recommended a psychological evaluation to determine Alex's overall intellectual capability and to assess his emotional as well as attentional functioning.

During the psychological evaluation, the evaluator made note of the fact that Alex created numerous projective stories about victimization. In the clinical interview, which involved short discussions over several days, Alex hesitantly reported that he had once witnessed his stepfather raping his mother. He stated that this had occurred 2 years earlier. This traumatic experience coincided with retrospective teacher reports of when Alex's symptoms emerged. For Alex, these symptoms were a warning sign of distress rather than of ADHD.

The school psychologist arranged for a meeting with Alex's mother and included Alex in the second half of the session. Alex's mother confirmed the event but denied that she had been aware that her son had witnessed it. The stepfather was no longer in the picture, and she tried to reassure Alex that everyone was now safe. Alex began crying and admitted that he had confronted his stepfather after the rape and that his stepfather had threatened to kill his mother if he ever told anyone. Clearly, Alex had had a lot to contend with during the 2-year period since the initial trauma. Alex, his mother, and his siblings entered family therapy. Later, his mother decided to file a police report. Alex expressed relief that he no longer had to carry the burden of this secret.

Alex displayed his traumatic response through symptoms of agitation, inattention, and sadness. Other maltreated children may display different responses. For example, Emily became sullen and argumentative, while Stephen became perfectionistic because he feared that poor school performance or errors could result in severe punishments at home.

Shonk and Cicchetti (2001) assert that maltreatment may make youngsters more vulnerable to many different disorders, such as those involving "externalizing and internalizing behavior problems" (p. 5). These investigators studied 146 maltreated children, of which "60.3% experienced emotional maltreatment, 86.5% were neglected, 58.7% had been physically abused, and 20.6% were sexually abused" (p. 6). These percentages suggest that some youngsters experienced more than one of these life stressors. The researchers found that the children's teachers rated these students as having more academic and social difficulties as well as lower "ego resiliency than comparison children" (p. 12). According to Shonk and Cicchetti (2001), "high ego resiliency" refers to having adaptive, healthy coping strategies when dealing with life's challenges (p. 5).

Trickett (1993) studied physically abused youngsters between the ages of 4 and 11, reporting that these children may struggle with depression and/or aggression, they may be withdrawn, and they may have academic struggles as well as social difficulties with both peers and adults. Furthermore, Trickett notes that a student's production on academic tasks that tap verbal skills may be negatively affected by abuse. The author speculates that this may occur "by producing in the child preoccupation with the abuse, reducing the child's sense of self-worth, inciting rebelliousness, and so forth" (p. 143).

The effect of maltreatment on the lives of children has also been investigated by Dodge, Lochman, Harnish, Bates, and Pettit (1997). They explored a symptom package that included "strikes back when teased, blames others in fights, and overreacts to accidents" (p. 39). They found that 41 percent of the sample of youngsters who had a history of physical abuse before the age of 6 displayed these difficulties. Far fewer children (15 percent) had the symptom cluster without this abuse history. In addition, the authors note that children who displayed this symptom cluster "were 3½ to 4 times as likely to be socially rejected as were other children" (p. 44). If a student displays symptoms such as those listed in Dodge and colleagues' symptom cluster, it does not necessarily mean that the child is a victim of abuse. However, these results suggest that abuse may increase the likelihood of a youngster displaying the symptoms.

It is not only victimization by actual physical abuse that can affect a child's behavior. Jouriles, Norwood, McDonald, Vincent, and Mahoney (1996) state that there is a positive correlation between "interpartner aggression, such as verbal threats and hitting objects" (p. 229) and children displaying behavioral difficulties.

Child Sexual Abuse. Child sexual abuse has also been specifically studied in the literature. Victims of this form of maltreatment have been shown to be susceptible to the development of posttraumatic stress disorder (PTSD) symptoms (Kendall-Tackett et al., 1993; Rodriguez, Ryan, Vande Kemp, & Foy, 1997). However, it is important for the reader to remember that not all children who have a history of abuse will develop this disorder or another specific manifestation of the trauma.

In a review of various studies on the effects of sexual abuse, Kendall-Tackett and colleagues (1993) report that PTSD, "poor self-esteem," "promiscuity," and behavioral difficulties were found to be evident in approximately one-third of victims (p. 167). Overall, symptoms varied depending on the age of the child. The authors note:

> For preschoolers, the most common symptoms were anxiety, nightmares, general PTSD, internalizing, externalizing, and inappropriate sexual behavior. For school-age children, the most common symptoms included fear, neurotic and general mental illness, aggression, nightmares, school problems, hyperactivity, and regressive behavior. For adolescents, the most common behaviors were depression; withdrawn, suicidal, or self-injurious behaviors; somatic complaints; illegal acts; running away, and substance abuse. (p. 167)

Kendall-Tackett and colleagues (1993) also report that sexual "molestations" were associated with a greater incidence of symptomatology when there was chronic abuse, an abuser who was intimately involved in the child's life, a history of repeated sexual abuse, and "use of force" (p. 171). If the victim, at the time of disclosure, had either a "negative outlook" or a negative "coping style" and/or if, at the time that the molestation was made public, the mother was not supportive, there was also an increased risk of symptom development (p. 171).

Suggestions for Teachers: Identifying and Helping Maltreated Children

Since some youngsters will not necessarily display overt symptoms and others will display a variety of difficulties that can reflect other causes, identifying victims of abuse or maltreatment can be an extremely complex task. Let us reflect back on our two case examples, Lisa and Evan. Lisa is sullen and withdrawn. She does not interact readily with her peers. On the surface, this may reflect symptoms that are consistent with abuse. Evan's agitation and challenging of his teacher could also reflect symptoms of trauma from an abusive relationship. How can one really know?

Teachers have a chance to get to know students over the course of an academic year. Sometimes young children will display their distress in drawings. For example, 8-year-old Angela drew pictures of a man throwing dishes at a woman. Although she may have been re-creating a scene she saw in a cartoon on television, she may also be re-creating a scene she actually witnessed in her personal life. Six-year-old Paul drew pictures of naked women, whom he had been exposed to by watching pornographic videotapes. Alert teachers should recognize these drawings as potentially indicative of a problem (although not necessarily of abuse) and consult the school mental health professional for information on appropriate ways to pursue the concern.

It is important not to make the child feel uncomfortable and to reassure the student that he or she is not bad and that the revelations will not get him or her into trouble with the teacher. However, there may be a realistic threat that breaking the silence about abuse might put the youngster at increased risk. The school mental health professional may request a personal consultation with the child or may want to meet with both the teacher and the student together to determine the most appropriate course of action. At times, the teacher, administrator, and/or mental health professional may need to call on the police or a child protection agency to investigate the situation.

A child who learns to trust a teacher may confide in that person. However, often the youngster is too guarded or apprehensive to do this directly. A withdrawn child may be encouraged to write notes to the teacher, since some students feel safer writing than speaking about concerns. The aggressive child may be given an opportunity to explore other means of communicating and to discuss why aggression seemed to be the mode of choice in response to particular situations; the teacher may provide examples of more effective, adaptive methods of response. In both of these examples, the student who was not abused could still benefit from the intervention.

If a child does confide abuse, or school personnel suspect abuse, it is essential that the administration be notified immediately and that the student be kept in school until it can be determined that sending the child home would not put him or her into a dangerous situation. Abuse/neglect reporting laws will also need to be followed.

After a 10-year-old student confided in her teacher about her physical abuse at home, the educator reported the information to the principal but added, "I really don't know what to do. If I tell her that I talked with you, she'll never trust me again. She doesn't want anyone else to know about the abuse." In reality, a teacher has little choice but to put physical safety over safeguarding a trusting relationship. The school mental health counselor can often guide a teacher on how to prepare the child for later interviews with child protective services, a welfare organization, or other individuals mandated to intervene without having the child feel completely unprotected and unduly frightened.

Abuse and neglect of children often bring out the protective instincts among teachers, who enter into the profession to assist and nurture students. It is important to remember that, despite the severity of symptoms or abuse, children will often maintain loyalty to their caregivers. Supporting a child, while not speaking too negatively about close family perpetrators, is a difficult task but one that may bring further comfort to a student.

To conclude, secrecy can allow abuse to continue in the home. Therefore, teachers should *always* consult the appropriate school personnel if suspicions arise about a student's being abused or neglected. The response to the suspicion should follow the procedures set out by the school board and school administration (e.g., reporting suspicions of abuse to school mental health staff or to appropriate protective organizations) and by the legal authorities who establish policies on reporting child abuse and neglect. In some instances, reports are made to outside agencies, yet no actual abuse or neglect has occurred. School staff are not obliged to investigate the allegation and confirm the maltreatment. Rather, the educators must report concerns if they have sufficient reason to suspect abuse or neglect.

School administrators can often guide teachers on when a concern warrants being reported to a protective agency. Ruby and Brigham (1997) stress that it may not always be easy to tell the difference between a child reporting real maltreatment and a child lying about maltreatment due to his or her own needs, being coached to lie, and/or due to the child's own fantasy life. If, however, all children's statements are doubted, some children may remain in extremely dangerous situations. To complicate matters even further, some children tell a story that does not seem to be believable even though actual maltreatment has occurred. Teachers should check with the administration and with the legal guidelines to determine when reporting of cases is mandated and when school personnel should initially follow up on statements at a building level.

The Effects of Divorce and Remarriage

In this section, research results regarding the effects of divorce and remarriage on children are reviewed. First, a specific example of how divorce can impact a child is presented.

DARRYL: PULLED IN TWO DIRECTIONS

Darryl is a 7-year-old boy whose parents are in the process of divorcing. Darryl's parents each scheduled a separate appointment with his teacher, Mrs. Roberts, to express an interest in helping Darryl adjust to the change. Through these two meetings, Mrs. Roberts felt that each parent wanted to negatively bias her opinion about Darryl's other parent. As legal issues in the divorce proceeded, Darryl frequently came to school looking tired and cried easily when something frustrated him. Mrs. Roberts also found that Darryl became more agitated and angry on Fridays; his parents had decided that Darryl would live in each home for a week at a time and switch off on Friday evenings.

Mrs. Roberts eventually consulted the school psychologist and learned that it is not uncommon for children of divorce to show reactions and that the school's group counseling program can often assist such students. After gaining permission from *both* parents, as suggested by the psychologist (who wanted Darryl to feel that his mother and his father supported the intervention group), Darryl willingly enrolled and was an active participant.

Research on the Effects of Divorce. How typical is Darryl's story? The research provides some answers. For instance, in a meta-analysis of published research, Amato and Keith (1991) found that the effects of divorce and other associated factors can negatively impact a child's sense of well-being, though these effects were noted to be "generally weak" (p. 40). Weaker effect sizes reflect less significant differences between groups (e.g., children of divorce and control groups).

In a more recent meta-analytic study of research on children of divorce, Amato (2001) reports that there was more sophisticated methodology in later studies than there had been in previous decades. Despite the methodological changes, Amato (2001) reports that more recent studies had similar findings to those done in previous decades, indicating that children of divorced parents showed significantly lower functioning in areas of "achievement, adjustment, and well-being" (p. 365) than did the children of parents who had remained married. The studies showed that boys of divorced parents tended to have a greater incidence of behavioral problems than did girls. Despite the noted differences, when the studies were more sophisticated, the findings were less significant, reflecting less difference between the groups.

It is not simply that the process of divorce creates negative adjustment of youngsters. For instance, Amato (2001) found that a youngster's response to a divorce is determined by many factors, such as "the level of conflict between the parents before and after separation, the quality of parenting . . . changes in the child's standard of living, and the number of additional stressors to which the children are exposed" (p. 366). In an earlier study, Kitzmann and Emery (1994) reported that those children who experience a parental divorce and then a continued state of parental conflict will manifest more behavioral problems than if there is a "decrease in the conflict during the first year" following the divorce (p. 156).

When reading information about the potential impact of divorce on children, it is helpful to keep in mind that sometimes youngsters have improved functioning once parents separate and no longer have intense conflicts. Children do not always show significant deterioration following divorce. I also know of students who have benefited from the use of art (e.g., drawing, acting, writing) as a therapeutic tool or entered psychotherapy to help them cope with the transition. Each child's response to divorce should be looked at based on the specific circumstances of the family, the child's personality, and other factors that might affect how the individual will cope.

MARK: SANDWICHED BETWEEN BATTLING PARENTS

Six-year-old Mark, for example, initially informed his teacher that he was happy about his parents' separation, since "they'll stop fighting and maybe love each other again." At that time, Mark did not understand the permanence of the separation, despite being told by his mother that a divorce was imminent. Mark did not show any overt negative effects of the separation until approximately 2 months later. At the time when his parents began fighting over the proposed divorce settlement, Mark found himself in the middle—sandwiched between the two people most important in his life and pulled in either direction by his mother and by his father. His father often asked Mark to "Tell your mother that . . . ," and his mother asked Mark to be the communicator back to his father.

It was after Mark became drawn into the battles that he began to display behavioral difficulties in school. He ripped up papers when he made mistakes, he yelled at children who were bothering him, and he frequently did not hand in his homework.

In support of the research findings already presented, the family disharmony and arguments correlated with Mark's behavioral issues. Mark found some solace in confiding in two of his older cousins and receiving support from them.

Wasserstein and La Greca (1996) note that there can be beneficial effects from positive peer support in coping with parental conflict. In their study of 51 boys and 45 girls from the fourth to the sixth grades who had two parents in the home, these authors report that their study results "supported the hypothesis that children who perceived their parents' marriage as more conflictual would exhibit higher levels of problem behaviors than those children who perceived their parents' marriage as less conflictual" (p. 181). However, the investigators found that if the children had significant support from close friends, then they did not typically demonstrate a significant increase in behavioral problems. It was those children who could not count on the support of friends and also encountered parental conflicts who demonstrated higher rates of behavioral difficulties. This not only indicates the importance of peer support but also raises questions about the negative effects of living in a home with two parents when a child perceives the parents as having a conflictual relationship.

Research on the Effects of Remarriage. Researchers have also investigated the effect of a parent's remarriage on the children. Hetherington (1993) studied and commented on this issue:

> In newly remarried families with preadolescent children, especially with daughters, a close marital relationship was associated with high levels of negative behavior from children toward both the mother and stepfather. For sons, this relationship was significant in the first 2 years of remarriage but not in later stages. For daughters, who were more likely than sons to have had a close, companionate relationship with their divorced mother, a satisfying marital relationship may be seen as more of a threat to continuation of an intimate mother-child relationship than it was to sons, who often were involved in coercive relationships with their divorced mothers. (p. 43)

Hetherington (1993) further notes that, for "preadolescents," if the stepfather made overtures toward building a close connection with the stepchild, while supporting the mother's disciplinary decisions, it increased the chances of the stepfather initially gaining the child's acceptance. However, Hetherington also states that adolescents tended to more quickly accept the stepfather when the stepfather took on the authoritative parental role from the onset.

Fine, Voydanoff, and Donnelly (1993) also investigated stepfamily dynamics. In their study, these researchers interviewed members of stepfamilies and asked participants to complete questionnaires. The findings lend support to the view that if a stepfather is an active disciplinarian when he first enters the family, there can be a risk of disrupting the family dynamics.

Bray (1992) proposed that if the new stepfamily includes "a good marital relationship characterized by high satisfaction, good communication, and more individuation," there will be an increased likelihood of the child being "more prosocial" and "better adjusted" (p. 66). Therefore, it is important to look at the individual stepfamily rather than to assume that all blended families will create similar stresses, distress, or positive rewards for the children. Cliff, for example, had been abandoned by his biological father years earlier and quickly embraced his new stepfamily without any apparent negative effects (except for the more typical parent–child issues that now arose with the presence of a second parent).

Suggestions for Teachers: Helping Students Affected by Divorce and Remarriage

If a teacher is aware that a child is experiencing a parental divorce or remarriage, is there anything that can be done to assist the student? As the research and our case example of Mark have illustrated, positive and supportive friendships can help a child as he or she copes with the family changes. In addition, I have witnessed the beneficial effects of positive parent–child relationships that continue during and after the stressful period of divorce. The close relationships may offer the youngster a sense of stability, security, and comfort. Therefore, perhaps a teacher can facilitate parent–child contact by inviting the parent into the class for an activity (if the student agrees and the other parent will support this plan) or can offer the student a chance to engage in a project that the parent may join in completing. However, since this places a potential burden on the parent, the mother's or father's approval should be obtained before the young student sets out to enlist their participation. This will hopefully safeguard the child from perceived rejection if the parent is unable or unwilling to help with the assignment.

Many schools now have group counseling for children of divorce. This may allow a child to realize that others share a similar experience and to find ways to accommodate to the new family living situation. Alpert-Gillis, Pedro-Carroll, and Cowen (1989) found that a group intervention program for children helped youngsters display increased adjustment to the parental divorce. These authors add that if the group program offers the children support, provides ways to cope with the feelings and problems that may arise from the divorce, and emphasizes the fact that there are many acceptable family constellations (giving them a better sense of their own family), then the program may increase the chances of a positive outcome for the participants.

Hetherington, Stanley-Hagan, and Anderson (1989) offer some comfort to divorcing parents and to those educators who encounter students in the process of a parental divorce. These authors remark that "many children eventually emerge from the divorce or remarriage of their parents as competent or even enhanced individuals" (p. 310). I have found that school remains the stable factor in many students' lives as their family changes and adjusts to a divorce or remarriage. The consistency of a teacher's classroom environment, positive peer friendships, an opportunity to discuss feelings or problems that might be upsetting the child, and close teacher–parent contact to allow for quick identification of a student's concerns may be helpful in minimizing the negative impact of this significant transition in a child's life. However, since some children are uncomfortable talking about family stress or knowing that school staff are aware of the divorce, the parent–teacher dialogue should be instituted in such a way that the child does not feel that this communication is an intrusion of the teacher into his or her personal world.

STRESS IN SCHOOL: BULLYING

While familial maltreatment and divorce affect the child at home, bullying can affect a student at school and have an impact on his or her emotional well-being and views toward academics and learning. This section discusses the victim, while Chapter 6 explores those who bully others. It should be noted, however, that there are times when a student is identified as both a victim and a bully. For instance, Forero, McLellan, Rissel, and Bauman (1999) studied 3,918 Australian students (aged approximately 12 to 16) and found that, over the course of the last school term, "21.5% were both bullied and bullied others on one or more occasions" (p. 344).

The Victims of School Bullying

Bullying in schools is not a new occurrence (Olweus, 1994), but it has received much coverage in the media in the last few years. Olweus (1994) defines the victim as a student who is "exposed, repeatedly and over time, to negative actions on the part of one or more other students. It is a negative action when someone intentionally inflicts, or attempts to inflict, injury or discomfort upon another" (p. 1173). Forero and colleagues (1999) state that 12.7 percent of their student sample reported being victimized by bullying, while Pellegrini, Bartini, and Brooks (1999) found data to suggest that the incidence may even be somewhat higher.

Research findings indicate that the incidence of *physical* bullying may decrease as a child's age increases (e.g., Olweus, 1994; Perry, Kusel, & Perry,

1988). Numerous research studies have investigated whether boys and girls are subject to different rates of bullying. For instance, Perry and colleagues (1988) and Kochenderfer-Ladd and Skinner (2002) report that girls and boys displayed similar risks of being victimized. Olweus (1994) suggests that there are two forms of bullying—direct and indirect—and that boys are more likely to experience the direct form of "bullying with relatively open attacks on the victim" (pp. 1175–1176), especially during the junior high school years, while girls and boys appeared to about equally experience the indirect form of bullying, which takes on a more subtle form. Olweus adds that bullying of girls was more likely to be carried out by boys rather than by girls.

BILL: HIS SECRET

Eleven-year-old Bill experienced victimization several times each week in school. Another student in his grade would knock books out of his hands, put Post-it stickers on his back with derogatory comments about him, and punch him in the arm if no adult was watching. Bill was also threatened with further physical harm if he did not bring the bully a snack every day at lunchtime. Bill's mother, unaware of the problem, noticed that her son was displaying increased fears, nightmares, social withdrawal, and low self-esteem. She had been told by her husband and friends that she was overprotective of Bill, so she initially believed that she was just imagining the concerns or that Bill was entering into preadolescence and that this new developmental stage might account for the change.

Bill felt uncomfortable telling adults about the bullying, because he felt that he should be able to cope with the difficulty himself. However, whenever he tried to confront the bully, Bill found himself crying and the bully laughing. Over time, Bill became so despondent that he began to think about suicide. Late one night, his mother found him crying in his room. At that point, Bill told her about his school difficulties. His mother and father met with his teacher and with the building principal the next day.

Immediately following this meeting, the school instituted several interventions that were moderately effective. His teacher developed a behavior-modification program for the grade level, where positive actions were reinforced. Each class on the grade level began an education program for students about ways to handle aggressive actions of others, alternatives to aggression (e.g., alternative coping strategies), and information about when to seek assistance from adults. In addition, Bill entered into school counseling to build his assertiveness skills and confidence. The principal also arranged for increased adult supervision during nonclassroom activities (e.g., recess, lunch, dismissal) and for formalized guidelines on how bullying behaviors were to be responded to by school personnel.

Although not all victims are going to exhibit suicidal ideation, intent, or plan, Kaltiala-Heino, Rimpela, Marttunen, Rimpela, and Rantanen (1999), who studied bullying among teenagers in Finland, discovered that depression and suicidal ideation existed among some of their sample. These authors note that there is a gender differentiation regarding suicidal ideation and bullying. "Among girls, severe suicidal ideation was associated with frequently being bullied or being a bully, and for boys it was associated with being a bully" (p. 349).

Hodges and Perry (1999) describe characteristics that they assert increase a student's chances of being a victim. They note that youngsters who cry easily, who are overtly anxiety ridden or apparently sad, and who are viewed as socially isolated may be victimized because of their perceived vulnerability. Physical weakness may also cause a student to appear vulnerable, and this will "no doubt furnish their attackers with greater reinforcement than stronger children do" (p. 683).

Olweus (1994) describes two subgroups of victims. He describes "submissive victim" (p. 1179) as

> more anxious and insecure than other students in general. Further, they are often cautious, sensitive, and quiet. When attacked by other students, they commonly react by crying (at least in the lower grades) and withdrawal . . . [and these victims tend to] suffer from low self-esteem . . . they often look upon themselves as failures and feel stupid, ashamed, and unattractive. (p. 1178)

Olweus (1994) refers to a second group of victims as "provocative victims" (p. 1179). This is a smaller group of victims who generally display "both anxious and aggressive reaction patterns" (p. 1179). Regarding this second group, Olweus reports that they frequently struggle with their concentration, may behave in a hyperactive fashion, and may act in ways that can cause others around them to become tense and irritated. Yet Hodges and Perry (1999) found that individuals who act in a provocative manner may not necessarily be victimized. This suggests that other factors may contribute to victimization. Therefore, it appears that further study of this issue is still warranted.

LISA AND EVAN: VICTIMS?

If we return to our two case examples, Lisa and Evan, they might fall easily into the two subgroups proposed by Olweus (1994). For instance, it is possible that Lisa could be a submissive victim, since she tends to withdraw and is quiet and sullen.

Evan, on the other hand, may be a provocative victim. His agitation and sarcastic manner of relating to fellow students may lead to anger among his peer group. Even if this is the case, it would not mean that Evan's behavior *caused* his victimization. It is important not to blame the victim for another's actions. Evan's teacher may want to take some time to assess how Evan's peers respond to him and whether he is the victim of any bullying. It may turn out that Evan is not experiencing bullying but just coincidentally displays the behavior that overlaps with Olweus's victim group.

Once again, the cases of Lisa and Evan highlight the fact that a child's behavior can point to distress, but the cause (and potential consequences associated with it) requires further investigation.

Indications of Vulnerability

What other signs might raise suspicions that a child is, or is not, vulnerable to bullying? There are several indications that having friends with "externalizing behaviors" (Hodges & Perry, 1999, p. 683) or "having bullies as friends" (Pellegrini et al., 1999, p. 223) may help minimize the victimization of a student whom a bully might tend to target.

Finnegan, Hodges, and Perry (1998) note that in boys it is possible to predict an increased chance of victimization when there is an overprotective mother. However, such a correlation is not noted for girls. The authors speculate that the overprotective mother diminishes the opportunity for the development of traits "such as independence and assertion" that can be important within the culture of young men (p. 1082). They found that girls who were victimized by their peers often perceived their mothers as "hostile and rejecting" (p. 1082). This perception of the mother may inhibit the girl's ability to relate easily and closely to her peers, which requires the development of a "need for communion" and "social skills" (p. 1082).

As Bill's case illustrated earlier, it is important for teachers and parents to be aware of victim–bully situations since there can be serious emotional consequences for a victim. For instance, in a review of studies that assessed the effects of bullying, Kochenderfer-Ladd and Skinner (2002) note that youngsters who have repeatedly been victimized by peers "are at risk for a variety of adjustment problems, including childhood depression, loneliness, anxiety, peer rejection, and school-related problems, including absenteeism and dropping out" (p. 267). Graham and Juvonen (1998) studied sixth- and seventh-grade students and found that those individuals "who perceive themselves as victimized are vulnerable to adjustment difficulties such as loneliness, social anxiety, and low self-worth" (p. 596).

Suggestions for Teachers: Helping Identified Victims

Olweus (1994) suggests that the school should be "characterized by warmth, positive interest, and involvement from adults, on the one hand, and firm limits to unacceptable behavior on the other" (p. 1185), with clear communication between school and home, close supervision during periods such as recess, class discussions about bullying and clear rules against it, and "serious talks with bullies" and with "victims" (p. 1186). Many of these intervention strategies were implemented to help Bill.

Although adults frequently encourage students to develop problem-solving strategies and to independently implement them, children may also need to be taught when teachers and/or parents should be sought out to help resolve a conflict. Newman, Murray, and Lussier (2001) note that children in elementary school who have experienced conflict with other youngsters are often hesitant to seek help from an adult. To them, seeking help is more to avoid a conflict than to resolve one. The authors comment that teachers should make it clear to students that adult help is available and should be sought in times of need. Newman and colleagues suggest that such an atmosphere may contribute to a safer school environment. It may also safeguard the lives of youngsters who become so despondent that death begins to look like a viable alternative to continued victimization and silent suffering.

In sum, victimization is neither a new nor an extraordinarily unusual occurrence. The effects can be significant, but the research literature suggests that interventions can have a positive impact. The intervention programs can be instituted in many different domains, such as the school environment, classroom structure, parent–child relationships, and individual assistance for the children. The intervention plan that was described earlier to help 11-year-old Bill reflects the use of multiple approaches to ameliorate the bullying situation.

ANXIETY AND ANXIETY DISORDERS

Defining Anxiety

The previous section discussed student victimization and the fact that it is not a rare occurrence. Similarly, it is not unusual for students to experience anxiety (Dadds et al., 1999; Huberty, 1987). However, unlike victimization, the presence of anxiety is not always found to be inherently dysfunctional. For instance, Huberty (1987) reports that there seems to be an optimal level of anxiety that motivates the individual rather than impeding his or her performance or ability to function. He notes that moderate levels of anxiety can have a positive effect on motivation.

Bouton, Mineka, and Barlow (2001) note that "anxiety prepares the system for an anticipated trauma" (p. 24), and Gillett (2001) reports that "it seems very likely that the capacity for anxiety arose through natural selection because of its obvious role in avoiding danger" (p. 269). When anxiety does not enable us, there are times when it hampers or even disables us. It is these situations that warrant further explanation here.

NINA AND VANESSA: NERVOUS

Eight-year-old Nina admitted to having mild feelings of nervousness about her role in a dance performance but denied that this was a concern and enthusiastically expressed excitement about the recital. However, standing next to Nina was her friend, Vanessa. Vanessa hid behind her mother's back as she stood off stage before the performance. Vanessa began crying and commented that she could not go onto the stage. In her case, the anxiety created uncomfortable levels of tension, fear, and uncertainty. Vanessa's mother was able to calm Vanessa's fears eventually, and Vanessa felt proud of her accomplishments during the recital, but she displayed anxiety that, without parental support, could have deprived her of the performance satisfaction experienced by Nina. Although Vanessa was able to overcome her initial anxiety, some children become quite disabled by it.

DARLENE: MORE THAN NERVOUS

Eight-year-old Darlene, for instance, was also scheduled to perform in the dance re-cital, but she cried most of the prior night, telling her parents that all the other chil-dren danced better than she did and that she felt "sick" when she thought about having to perform the next day. Darlene did not attend the dance recital. Her response to this event was characteristic of her reluctance to attend other social gatherings, such as birthday parties. Eventually, Darlene's parents brought Darlene for a psychologi-cal evaluation. She was diagnosed as suffering from a social phobia and benefited from a treatment program.

According to Dadds and colleagues (1999), "Anxiety problems are the most common form of psychological distress by children and adolescents" (p. 145). Anxiety can be a complex state that may include "affective, behav-ioral, physiological, and cognitive components" (Silverman, La Greca, & Wasserstein, 1995, p. 671).

There are numerous fears and anxieties displayed by children, such as those seen in some cases of posttraumatic stress disorder (see Chapter 3). For some youngsters, the emotional discomfort can take the form of sepa-ration anxiety, anticipatory anxiety, social anxiety, and so forth. In their study of children, Silverman and colleagues (1995) found that "the three most common areas of worry reported by children in . . . [their] sample con-cerned School, Health, and Personal Harm" (p. 682). Despite the fact that the sample of youngsters in this study was from a school that was not lo-cated in a community with a high incidence of crime, the most frequent concerns expressed by these children were fears of being attacked by oth-ers and of bodily injury or harm.

In her study of children, Spence (1997) concludes that some characteristics of anxiety may change based on a child's age. Her research shows that the symptoms of obsessions, compulsions, and separation anxiety are more likely to be reported by younger than by older children. Ollendick and King (1994) also studied the effect of one's age on the nature of anxiety. They comment that in the younger child "separation anxiety disorder and simple phobia are more prevalent . . . [while] older children and adolescents" are more likely to have depressive disorders, overanxious disorders, and social phobias (p. 922).

In the following pages, a variety of anxiety disorders that affect children are reviewed. The term *phobia* is used to refer to a fear that is not statistically validated as a realistic danger (e.g., fear of flying, fear of spiders).

Social Phobias

Let us revisit the case of Darlene, who was overwhelmed by her fear of social situations, refused to participate in a dance recital, and felt too uncomfortable to attend birthday parties. Her fear was not based on realistic danger, since the actual situations were well supervised and deemed to be safe by the adults and by many of the children around her. Children, such as Darlene, who suffer from social phobias may not be globally handicapped. In fact, these youngsters may do quite well in situations that a socially confident child may fear, since the social fear does not necessarily generalize to all of life's situations (e.g., test taking, playing with a large dog).

However, Spence, Donovan, and Brechman-Toussaint (1999) studied children with social phobias and found that they "tended to anticipate negative outcomes from social-evaluative situations, evaluated their own performance more negatively, and showed a higher level of negative cognitions in relation to social-evaluative tasks [than did other youngsters]" (p. 219).

These authors also report that children who do not suffer from a social phobia appear to have more adaptive social skills than their socially phobic counterparts. Spence and colleagues conclude that phobic youngsters may minimize their social interactions and, therefore, have less opportunity to practice and develop social skills. With less developed skills, their level of social phobia increases, causing a "vicious cycle" (p. 219). If past social skill failures and fear of embarrassment, ridicule, and/or humiliation created the anxiety and the wish to avoid socially disappointing situations in the future, then social skills training may be useful to boost skills and confidence.

Separation Anxiety

Some students may display separation anxiety. This can involve anxiety over separating from a parent to go to school, separating from a teacher to go to the playground, or separating from a trusted friend to go to a different activity. According to the American Psychiatric Association (APA) (2000), a person with a separation anxiety disorder may have numerous symptoms, such as "recurrent excessive distress" (p. 121) upon separation from the trusted person or environment, may worry about the safety of trusted others when they are not around, may have "nightmares," and may have somatic complaints. The discomfort must be evident for "at least 4 weeks" (p. 125) to qualify for the diagnosis.

MITCHELL: SEPARATION ANXIETY OR DEFIANCE?

At times a child may camouflage separation anxiety by appearing to be defiant or rebellious. For instance, 9-year-old Mitchell had always experienced some anxiety when he had to leave his mother to go to school. His mother was a single parent, and Mitchell believed that it was his role to protect her. He feared that she would need him and he would be in school and, thus, not around to help her. After a recent summer vacation, Mitchell felt a resurgence of anxiety about 1 week prior to the start of the new school year. By the time school began, Mitchell was having nightmares of people chasing his mother and he had lost his appetite. Although he was reluctant to go to school on the first day, he was happy to see his friends once he arrived. However, he admitted—only to himself—that he almost cried when his mother said goodbye and ushered him onto the school bus.

On the second day of school, Mitchell reflected on how long he would be at school and, thus, away from his mother. His anxiety overwhelmed him, and he told his mother that he was sick and could not go to school. His concerned mother took his temperature, found it to be normal, and coaxed him to get ready to get on the bus. At that point, Mitchell began crying. Rather than admit to feeling nervous (which he was embarrassed about and felt would lead to his mother's disappointment in him), Mitchell shouted through his tears: "I hate school. I don't learn anything. The teacher is stupid. The kids are stupid. I'm not going any more."

Mitchell's mother sent him to his room so that she could have time to think about the dilemma and how she might encourage Mitchell to voluntarily go to school. Despite Mitchell's protestations, his mother knew him well enough to realize that he was shouting from fear rather than from hatred of school. She phoned Mitchell's teacher and explained the problem. His teacher and mother developed a plan to ease the separation anxiety. That evening, Mitchell's mother reassured her son that she was fine and that she was busy taking care of responsibilities during the day so that she could spend more time with him when he returned from school. She hoped that this would ease any concerns that Mitchell had about her ability to function independently from him. She then began the plan that was developed with the teacher's input.

For the first few days, Mitchell's mother walked him to the school building, then she spent a few days walking him to the corner of the block where the school was located, and then to a friend's house so that Mitchell and his friend could take the bus together. By that point, Mitchell had had some time to develop a relationship with his teacher and the separation concern decreased. The teacher had helped Mitchell by quickly engaging him in an activity when he entered the school building each day and by allowing him to sit next to a friend in class. Soon, Mitchell no longer worried excessively about his mother and was able to enjoy the school experience.

Unfortunately, not all children with separation anxiety respond as quickly, and with as little intervention, as Mitchell. Sometimes in-school counseling, private psychotherapy, or a psychiatric consultation may be indicated. In addition, sometimes prolonging the goodbye period (e.g., having the parent walk the child to school) can increase a child's anticipatory anxiety about the eventual separation. Therefore, each child's needs should be assessed on an individual basis.

Other Phobias and Disorders Related to Anxiety

A Specific Phobia. This phobia reflects a narrow area of distressing anxiety, but it can have a significant impact on a person's daily functioning if the feared object or event is prevalent in one's life. For instance, a snake charmer who suddenly develops a phobia about reptiles may lose his job because of this fear. However, a student with the identical fear who is in a class without snakes may appear to be a typical child without apparent anxieties. The American Psychiatric Association (2000) highlights some examples of specific phobias, including fears of "animals . . . heights . . . enclosed places" and so on (p. 445).

Overanxious Disorder of Childhood. In this disorder, according to the American Psychiatric Association (2000), a person has "excessive anxiety and worry . . . occurring more days than not for a period of at least 6 months" (p. 472), and the person may experience "restlessness, being easily fatigued, . . . [and other symptoms such as] irritability, muscle tension, (or) disturbed sleep" (p. 472). The anxiety displayed in this disorder creates "clinically significant distress" (American Psychiatric Association, 2000, p. 476).

Agoraphobia. Agoraphobia involves "anxiety about being in places or situations from which escape might be difficult (or embarrassing) or in which help may not be available in the event of having a Panic Attack . . . or panic-like symptoms" (APA, 2000, p. 432). Bouton and colleagues (2001) state that agoraphobia "literally refers to fear of the marketplace" (p. 5). The *agora* (in the word *agoraphobia*) refers to the open marketplace of early Greece and, therefore, agoraphobia can also be defined as a fear of open spaces.

"Agoraphobic avoidance behavior is simply one of the learned consequence of having severe unexpected panic attacks" (Bouton et al., 2001, p. 5).
The avoidance behavior can occur after a panic attack or after a series of
such attacks; the person attempts to avoid the symptoms by avoiding the
situation associated with their emergence. One individual, for instance, experienced panic while walking from her home to a nearby store. She unex-
pectedly began to develop sweaty palms, physical agitation, and racing
thoughts of impending disaster. Subsequently, she avoided leaving her house
to go to the store or to go anywhere else alone because of this episode and
fear of its recurrence.

Panic Disorder. A panic disorder, according to Bouton and colleagues (2001),
involves the experience of numerous "panic attacks that occur without any
obvious cues or triggers" (p. 5). The lives of those suffering from this difficulty, according to these authors, can be dramatically and negatively affected
when, in the most severe forms, the anxiety and panic lead to avoidance
behavior and the frequent complication of agoraphobia.

Other areas of anxiety may include those due to physiological causes,
those related to an obsessive–compulsive disorder (see Chapter 5), and those
that may not reach the level of a disorder or handicap but can create discomfort (e.g., the child is capable of taking tests in class but becomes uncomfortable and moderately anxious beforehand).

LISA AND EVAN: SAD? AGITATED? ANXIOUS?

Let us return to our two case examples, Lisa and Evan. Lisa is sad, sullen, and socially
withdrawn. Could she be suffering from an anxiety disorder? Although many children
will confide their anxiety to trusted adults, this is not always the case. If Lisa's teacher,
Mrs. Kane, suspected that Lisa might be overwhelmed by her fears or anxiety, then
she might want to gently ask Lisa if there is anything that is making her feel uncomfortable. Mrs. Kane might also contact Lisa's mother to see if further light could be
shed on why Lisa appears to be withdrawn. At times, a phobic person will expend so
much effort to look as if the situation is not overwhelming that he or she will have
little energy left to focus on work, friendships, or activities.

Our other case example, Evan, presents with symptoms of agitation (e.g., physical
restlessness), directly challenges his teacher, and is frequently late to school. His teacher,
Mrs. Lerner, wonders why Evan began arriving to school 15 minutes late, on a regular
basis, following the first few weeks of school. At the same time as his latenesses began,
his attitude changed. He became sarcastic and was no longer completing his assignments. Here again, anxiety cannot be ruled out as a cause of the change. Perhaps Evan
is coming to school late because he is ridden with fears each morning about leaving
home or about something that he will encounter in school. He may then resent school,

since he may see it as the root of his tension, so he displays his anger and agitation behaviorally. Mrs. Lerner may gain insight from studying the times that Evan acts disruptively, leaves the room, and comes to school particularly late or on time. Finding correlations between his behavior and events in his life may allow Mrs. Lerner to determine patterns and then, hopefully, narrow down the potential cause(s).

Help for Anxiety Disorders

Brief Group Therapy Intervention. Dadds and colleagues (1999) looked at the benefits of a group counseling program where children learned to gradually face feared situations or stimuli while receiving group support. Results indicated that this "brief psychosocial intervention has potential to prevent children with mild to moderate anxiety problems from developing more serious anxiety disorders over a 2-year period" (p. 148) and that while "girls tended to improve less than boys at posttreatment," the "effect disappeared at 24 months" (p. 149). The authors do caution, however, that youngsters with more severe forms of anxiety may not show as much improvement during and immediately following intervention.

Cognitive-Behavioral Therapy. Silverman and colleagues (1999) found that both self-control (e.g., cognitive strategies) and contingency management (e.g., behavioral conditioning) treatment were effective interventions in helping children overcome phobias. Ollendick and King (1994) report that treatment methods, "especially behavioral and cognitive-behavioral" (p. 923), have been found to be beneficial in helping children to overcome their anxiety in the short term and often for more prolonged periods.

A Few Words About Treatment Modalities. I have found that numerous forms of intervention can be successful. Some children have responded positively to insight-oriented psychodynamic treatment, others to cognitive-behavioral therapy, others to family-oriented interventions, and so forth. At times, combining various treatment modalities can produce highly beneficial results. An example can illustrate this point.

JAMES: SEPARATION ANXIETY AND PANIC ATTACKS

Eight-year-old James had a long history of separation anxiety and panic attacks. His symptoms emerged in kindergarten as he cried each night before school and each morning as he prepared for his day. James displayed social withdrawal in school, cried easily when his routine was changed, and refused to leave his teacher to go to lunch and special activities. In fact, James spent many hours in the principal's office during his early school years because he felt safe enough in the principal's presence to eat his lunch and remain in school.

James began meeting with the school psychologist on a regular basis at the end of kindergarten. He was aware of the fact that other children did not experience the same intensity of fears, and he expressed motivation to find a way to participate in his school program without overwhelming anxiety. James's counseling involved educating him (e.g., about the physiological effects of his anxiety and how it is not dangerous; about the immediate positive but long-term negative effects of avoiding situations that are unrealistically frightening him); educating his mother about the disorder; teaching James relaxation techniques; talking with James about thought stopping; developing a hierarchy of increasingly fearful events, which he agreed to slowly conquer through cognitive-behavioral techniques; and identifying his feelings and how a few events in his early life left him fearing losing control in his world. This latter discussion revealed how certain situations—such as his mother arriving an hour late to pick him up once from a baby-sitter, when he was 4—left him feeling vulnerable and out of control. In this instance, James appeared to be most upset by his baby-sitter's anger at his mother's lateness.

The teacher was also involved in James's treatment plan. His teacher joined several counseling sessions to support James in his efforts to participate in school, to reassure him that he would not be forced to do something that made him too anxious, and to let him know that she firmly believed that the activities that students were involved with during the day were safe. The teacher was instructed not to try to debate with James, however, about whether his fears were realistic, since this could leave him feeling unsupported and defensive.

When James learned that he could leave stressful situations if he needed to (but only for 10-minute periods) and go to the principal's office or to the psychologist's office, this reduced some of his anxiety. However, with another child this could reinforce negative coping strategies of withdrawal and avoidance. James worked hard to better understand his feelings, his physical reactions to stress, and his priorities. He eventually participated fully in his school activities and enjoyed developing positive peer relationships.

Suggestions for Teachers: Helping Students with Anxiety

Each student will probably require an individualized intervention plan since the form of anxiety, root of anxiety, and motivation to change vary. If a teacher is aware that a child is anxious, it is often important to gather information from the parent to determine how the child has successfully coped in other situations. Sometimes a child can generate strategies to ease stress that are easily implemented in school (e.g., a kindergartner who brings a stuffed animal to school but leaves it in his backpack all day).

In severe cases of childhood anxiety, the mental health professional in the building could guide the teacher on how much to *give in* to the fears and how much to hold on to high expectations for adaptive behaviors from the student. The mental health professional can also offer suggestions about when it is appropriate to recommend a formal evaluation; for instance, some learning disabled children feel so nervous about school competence that they develop anxiety reactions to academic situations in which they expect to be called upon to perform. The mental health professional may also recommend counseling, therapy, or a psychiatric consultation. Since there appears to be "comorbidity of anxiety disorders with affective disorders" (Ollendick & King, 1994, p. 922), a student may need to be clinically assessed to clarify the specific nature of the disorder or disorders. Proper intervention could then be instituted.

CONCLUSION

To conclude, this chapter addressed some environmental issues that may create stress for students (e.g., maltreatment, divorce, birth of a sibling, changes, bullying) as well as information on the internalized disorders of anxiety. Because disorders and causes may overlap, a clear determination of a child's distress can be a complex process. A learning disability may create feelings of uncertainty in one child, a medical issue may create physiological changes similar to panic attacks and lead to anxiety in another student, and a social skills deficit and social skills failures may lead to social anxiety in a third youngster. In addition, students may appear to be anxious but actually are suffering from another disorder (e.g., agitated depression).

The teacher who can identify that a child is struggling has made a positive move to eventually helping that student. If child–teacher and parent–teacher contacts do not provide clear paths for problem identification and intervention, and creating a supportive, predictable, nurturing classroom environment does not provide comfort to the child, then the teacher may consider consulting the school-based team of specialists for advice and support.

REFERENCES

Alpert-Gillis, L. J., Pedro-Carroll, J. L., & Cowen, E. L. (1989). The children of divorce intervention program: Development, implementation, and evaluation of a program for young urban children. *Journal of Consulting and Clinical Psychology, 57*(5), 583–589.

Amato, P. R. (2001). Children of divorce in the 1990s: An update of the Amato and Keith (1991) meta-analysis. *Journal of Family Psychology, 15*(3), 355–370.

Amato, P. R., & Keith, B. (1991). Parental divorce and the well-being of children: A meta-analysis. *Psychological Bulletin, 110*(1), 26–46.

American Psychiatric Association (APA) (2000). *Diagnostic and statistical manual of mental disorders: Fourth edition, DSM-IV-TR, text revision.* Washington, DC: Author.

Bouton, M. E., Mineka, S., & Barlow, D. H. (2001). A modern learning theory perspective on the etiology of panic disorder. *Psychological Review, 108*(1), 4–32.

Bray, J. H. (1992). Family relationships and children's adjustment in clinical and nonclinical stepfather families. *Journal of Family Psychology, 6*(1), 60–68.

Dadds, M. R., Holland, D. E., Laurens, K. R., Mullins, M., Barrett, P. M., & Spence, S. H. (1999). Early intervention and prevention of anxiety disorders in children: Results at 2–year follow-up. *Journal of Consulting and Clinical Psychology, 67*(1), 145–150.

Dodge, K. A., Lochman, J. E., Harnish, J. D., Bates, J. E., & Pettit, G. S. (1997). Reactive and proactive aggression in school children and psychiatrically impaired chronically assaultive youth. *Journal of Abnormal Psychology, 106*(1), 37–51.

Fine, M. A., Voydanoff, P., & Donnelly, B. W. (1993). Relations between parental control and warmth and child well-being in stepfamilies. *Journal of Family Psychology, 7*(2), 222–232.

Finnegan, R. A., Hodges, E., & Perry, D. G. (1998). Victimization by peers: Associations with children's reports of mother-child interaction. *Journal of Personality and Social Psychology, 75*(4), 1076–1086.

Forero, R., McLellan, L., Rissel, C., & Bauman, A. (1999). Bullying behaviour and psychosocial health among school students in New South Wales, Australia: Cross-sectional survey. *British Medical Journal, 319*, 344–348.

Gillett, E. (2001). Signal anxiety from the adaptive point of view. *Psychoanalytic Psychology, 18*(2), 268–286.

Graham, S., & Juvonen, J. (1998). Self-blame and peer victimization in middle school: An attributional analysis. *Developmental Psychology, 34*(3), 587–599.

Hetherington, E. M. (1993). An overview of the Virginia Longitudinal Study of Divorce and Remarriage with a focus on early adolescence. *Journal of Family Psychology, 7*(1), 39–56.

Hetherington, E. M., Stanley-Hagan, M., & Anderson, E. R. (1989). Marital transitions: A child's perspective. *American Psychologist, 44*(2), 303–312.

Hodges, E., & Perry, D. G. (1999). Personal and interpersonal antecedents and consequences of victimization by peers. *Journal of Personality and Social Psychology, 76*(4), 677–685.

Huberty, T. J. (1987). Children and anxiety. In A. Thomas & J. Grimes (Eds.), *Children's needs: Psychological perspectives* (pp. 45–51). Washington, DC: National Association of School Psychologists.

Jouriles, E. N., Norwood, W. D., McDonald, R., Vincent, J. P., & Mahoney, A. (1996). Physical violence and other forms of marital aggression: Links with children's behavior problems. *Journal of Family Psychology, 10*(2), 223–234.

Kaltiala-Heino,, R., Rimpela, M., Marttunen, M., Rimpela, A., & Rantanen, P. (1999). Bullying, depression, and suicidal ideation in Finnish adolescents: School survey. *British Medical Journal, 319*, 348–351.

Kendall-Tackett, K. A., Williams, L. M., & Finkelhor, D. (1993). Impact of sexual abuse on children: A review and synthesis of recent empirical studies. *Psychological Bulletin, 113*(1), 164–180.

Kitzmann, K. M., & Emery, R. E. (1994). Child and family coping one year after mediated and litigated child custody disputes. *Journal of Family Psychology, 8*(2), 150–159.

Kochenderfer-Ladd, B., & Skinner, K. (2002). Children's coping strategies: Moderators of the effects of peer victimization? *Developmental Psychology, 38*(2), 267–278.

Kramer, L., & Gottman, J. M. (1992). Becoming a sibling: "With a little help from my friends." *Developmental Psychology, 28*(4), 685–699.

Newman, R. S., Murray, B., & Lussier, C. (2001). Confrontation with aggressive peers at school: Students' reluctance to seek help from the teacher. *Journal of Educational Psychology, 93*(2), 398–410.

Ollendick, T. H., & King, N. J. (1994). Diagnosis, assessment, and treatment of internalizing problems in children: The role of longitudinal data. *Journal of Consulting and Clinical Psychology, 62*(5), 918–927.

Olweus, D. (1994). Annotation: Bullying at school: Basic facts and effects of a school based intervention program. *Journal of Child Psychology and Psychiatry, 35*(7), 1171–1190.

Pellegrini, A. D., Bartini, M., & Brooks, F. (1999). School bullies, victims, and aggressive victims: Factors relating to group affiliation and victimization in early adolescence. *Journal of Educational Psychology, 91*(2), 216–224.

Perry, D. G., Kusel, S. J., & Perry, L. C. (1988). Victims of peer aggression. *Developmental Psychology, 24*(6), 807–814.

Rodriguez, N., Ryan, S. W., Vande Kemp, H., & Foy, D. W. (1997). Posttraumatic stress disorder in adult female survivors of childhood sexual abuse: A comparison study. *Journal of Consulting and Clinical Psychology, 65*(1), 53–59.

Ruby, C. L., & Brigham, J. C. (1997). The usefulness of the criteria-based content analysis technique in distinguishing between truthful and fabricated allegations. *Psychology, Public Policy, and Law, 3*(4), 705–737.

Shonk, S. M., & Cicchetti, D. (2001). Maltreatment, competency deficits, and risk for academic and behavioral maladjustment. *Developmental Psychology, 37*(1), 3–17.

Silverman, W. K., Kurtines, W. M., Ginsburg, G. S., Weems, C. F., Rabian, B., & Serafini, L. T. (1999). Contingency management, self-control, and education support in the treatment of childhood phobic disorders: A randomized clinical trial. *Journal of Consulting and Clinical Psychology, 67*(5), 675–687.

Silverman, W. K., La Greca, A. M., & Wasserstein, S. (1995). What do children worry about? Worries and their relation to anxiety. *Child Development, 66*, 671–686.

Spence, S. H. (1997). Structure of anxiety symptoms among children: A confirmatory factor-analytic study. *Journal of Abnormal Psychology, 106*(2), 280–297.

Spence, S. H., Donovan, C., & Brechman-Toussaint, M. (1999). Social skills, social outcomes, and cognitive features of childhood social phobia. *Journal of Abnormal Psychology, 108*(2), 211–221.

Trickett, P. K. (1993). Maladaptive development of school-aged, physically abused children: Relationships with the child-rearing context. *Journal of Family Psychology, 7*(1), 134–147.

Wasserstein, S. B., & La Greca, A. M. (1996). Can peer support buffer against behavioral consequences of parental discord? *Journal of Clinical Child Psychology, 25*(2), 177–182.

CHAPTER 5

Other Internalized Disorders and the Mind–Body Interaction

Obsessive Thoughts; Compulsive Behaviors;
Obsessive-Compulsive Disorder; Perfectionism;
Depression; Mind–Body Interaction;
The Impact of Chronic Medical Concerns

At the end of the last chapter, various forms of anxiety disorders were reviewed. Anxiety is an internalized disorder, since the primary symptoms involve thoughts or feelings. In this chapter, other internalized disorders are explored, along with a discussion of how the mind and body interact and how a prolonged illness may affect a student's school life.

OBSESSIVE THOUGHTS

At times, many people experience a brief or mild obsessive focus. This obsessive preoccupation could take the form of having a song running through one's head throughout the day after hearing it early in the morning, worrying whether one turned off the stove before leaving home, or even being preoccupied with concerns about safety. Very young children sometimes are described as fixated on a particular topic when they repeatedly and insistently ask their parents questions such as "But *why* is the sky blue? Tell me!"

Not all repetitive thoughts and periods of intense focus are dysfunctional. For instance, if Albert Einstein had been less focused on his professional interest, would the world have learned about the theory of relativity so quickly? If Ben Franklin had not shown an intense interest in electricity, would the world have advanced technologically in the same time period? Sometimes, the ability to *obsessively focus* on a goal is quite functional and can be described as persistence and as a positive drive to excel. However, there are times when a preoccupation or obsessive thought can be detrimental.

MELISSA AND HARRY: PREOCCUPIED

Nine-year-old Melissa had difficulty focusing on the class lessons and on her classwork because she was frequently preoccupied by her concern that she must stay calm or she might *explode* and hurt someone. Melissa did not have a history of rages or atypical expressions of aggression, nor had she directly witnessed excessive anger on the part of others. Despite her history, Melissa tried to avoid all frustration and stress in order to minimize her chances of experiencing angry feelings.

Six-year-old Harry also had difficulty listening in class, and his teacher reported that he often seemed to be daydreaming. One day, Harry hesitantly informed his mother that "I just can't stop thinking about you when I'm supposed to be doing my work at school. I get worried that you are sick or something." Harry's mother was in good health, but this information neither calmed Harry's anxiety nor lessened his fixation on his mother's physical well-being. Both Harry and Melissa could be described as obsessing about specific concerns.

COMPULSIVE BEHAVIORS

In this chapter, the dysfunctional obsessive characteristics that are often associated with an obsessive–compulsive disorder are explored. First, however, it is important not only to understand how obsessions are displayed but also to examine the many ways in which compulsive features can be manifested.

KEVIN AND SUZANNA: SUFFERING FROM COMPULSIVE ACTIONS

Ten-year-old Kevin was frequently late for school because of his extremely ritualistic morning routine. He needed to get out of bed with his right foot first and he had to immediately open his homework book to make sure that he had, in fact, completed the work the prior evening. Then he packed up his backpack, arranging books in a particular order, before he attended to his hygiene needs. Each part of his morning was ritualized, including how many bites of food he ate before he drank some milk. If he had to deviate from this routine, he became irritable and anxious. Yet Kevin knew that his friends probably had fewer routines each morning than he had created for himself. Punctuality was not part of his compulsion, so being late to class did not create undue anxiety for him.

Suzanna could also be described as having compulsive characteristics. However, her compulsive actions intruded minimally on her daily life. The compulsive behaviors emerged immediately prior to any writing activity. She felt that it was important to arrange items on her desk in a particular way, then push in her chair, and then tap each finger twice on the desk before starting the assignment. Suzanna understood that the actions had no rational connection to increased creativity, but she felt too anxious to write without first engaging in these compulsive behaviors.

Compulsive behaviors can range in intensity and can be quite dysfunctional, minimally problematic, or even beneficial at times. Superstitious behaviors sometimes fall into the category of being compulsive. If a person must cross the street every time he or she sees a black cat, this is a ritualistic response and can be viewed as compulsive.

Some compulsive behaviors can be adaptive. A busy manager who always makes sure that messages are returned that day and that tasks are put into priority order each night so that they can be handled properly the following morning may be described as compulsive, yet he or she might just be well organized and efficient. The school nurse who always stops to put on gloves before cleaning off blood from injured students' scraped knees and the mother who makes sure to wash her hands after tending to her sick child will probably benefit from the inflexible routines that they have established. However, 10-year-old Jamal washes his hands several times an hour, despite the fact that he is not exposed to unusually high-risk situations. For him, this compulsive behavior interferes with his ability to focus on his schoolwork and makes him stand out from his peers as being different.

OBSESSIVE–COMPULSIVE DISORDER (OCD)

Defining OCD

When focusing on certain thoughts or engaging in particular behaviors over and over again becomes "excessive or unreasonable," it may indicate that a child or adult is suffering from an obsessive–compulsive disorder (OCD) (American Psychiatric Association [APA], 2000, p. 457). In OCD, a person may experience obsessions, or compulsions, or both. Swedo and Rapoport (1989) state that "obsessive–compulsive disorder is a disease of rational irrationality. Children with OCD know that their actions are 'crazy'" (p. 130). The authors add that these children often try to hide their symptoms from others and may not admit to needing assistance in dealing with the disorder. However, the American Psychiatric Association (2000) reports that some children may not have the insight to know that their OCD symptoms are dysfunctional or unnecessary, yet they can still meet the criteria for this disorder if the symptom presentation is consistent with this diagnosis.

The American Psychiatric Association (2000) describes OCD obsessions as

> persistent ideas, thoughts, impulses, or images that are experienced as intrusive and inappropriate and that cause marked anxiety or distress . . . [and the] most common obsessions are repeated thoughts about contamination . . .

repeated doubts . . . a need to have things in a particular order . . . aggressive or horrific impulses . . . and sexual imagery. (p. 457)

Swedo and Rapoport (1989) comment that "most of the obsessive thoughts fall into one of three categories: fear of harm, illness or death; fear of doing wrong or having done wrong; [and] fear of contamination" (p. 139). These authors also note that compulsions about cleaning and washing are the most typical ones found in youngsters who have an obsessive–compulsive disorder.

According to the American Psychiatric Association (2000), OCD compulsions may include

repetitive behaviors . . . or mental acts (e.g., praying, counting, repeating words silently) the goal of which is to prevent or reduce anxiety or distress . . . [and the] most common compulsions involve washing and cleaning, counting, checking, requesting or demanding assurances, repeating actions, and ordering. (p. 457)

The Research

OCD is not an unusually rare disorder. In fact, the American Psychiatric Association (2000) suggests that 2.5 percent of the population may experience the disorder at some point over the course of their lifetime. In a review of the literature on this disorder, Hanna (1995) reports that OCD can be found across different cultures and that children with the disorder appear to have symptoms that are very similar to those of their adult counterparts with the same disorder.

OCD can appear in very young children, even as young as 4, according to Swedo and Rapoport (1989). Although the incidence of OCD is reported to be equal for both genders (American Psychiatric Association, 2000), males seem to exhibit the initial symptoms of the disorder at younger ages than do their female counterparts (American Psychiatric Association, 2000; Hanna, 1995). The number and nature of obsessions and compulsions may vary over a period of time for those afflicted with the disorder (Hanna, 1995).

Leonard and colleagues (1989) reflect on the origins of OCD, using a historical perspective. They comment that the OCD "routines that deal with cleanliness, danger, doubt, and guilt, supports [sic] the concept of preprogrammed behaviors most probably developed over evolutionary time at a level of complexity previously unimaginable in humans" (p. 1092). These routines may have helped to ward off illness and danger and promote a positive societal atmosphere.

Some research suggests a biological-physiological component to the disorder. For instance, Savage and colleagues (2000) report that there is significant support in the literature "that OCD is associated with distinct patterns of brain dysfunction and cognitive impairment" (p. 141). Swedo and Rapoport (1989) also reviewed the literature and state that studies of the brain using PET scans (positron emission tomography) have noted some atypical physiological findings in OCD patients. PET scan results "show an increase in metabolic activity in the frontal lobes, caudate nucleus, and cingulate gyrus of obsessive–compulsive patients, . . . supporting a basal ganglia-frontal lobe model of OCD" (p. 151). The American Psychiatric Association (2000) reports that there are higher rates of this disorder in identical versus fraternal twins; this further raises the suspicion of an interaction between mind and body in the manifestation of OCD symptoms.

Diagnosing OCD

Diagnosing OCD in a child is not always a simple task. For instance, some children do not appear to suffer from obsessions and/or compulsions in school because they work hard to contain the symptoms in that setting. Yet they do have the disorder and display the difficulties at home and in other situations. Once an accurate diagnosis is made, appropriate treatment (e.g., cognitive-behavioral therapy; medication) has often been found to be beneficial (Franklin, Abramowitz, Bux, Zoellner, & Feeny, 2002; Rapoport, Leonard, Swedo, & Lenane, 1993; Swedo & Rapoport, 1989).

While OCD may coexist with other conditions and areas of challenge, some of the symptoms of OCD can overlap with characteristics of other disorders (e.g., Asperger's disorder) and lead to a misdiagnosis. A precise diagnosis often requires a thorough mental health assessment. Research suggests that there may be some characteristics associated with the disorder. Savage and colleagues (2000), for instance, studied individuals with OCD and noted that they may adhere to a particular approach, or to a particular mindset, rather than having the cognitive flexibility to switch responses based upon nebulous circumstances. These authors also state that those with OCD may look at small details of a situation while overlooking the gestalt, or bigger picture.

SUSAN: OCD IN THE CLASSROOM

Perhaps 8-year-old Susan can help illustrate the findings of Savage and colleagues' (2000) study. Susan's teacher, Mr. Healy, reported that she is a bright, inquisitive student who is well behaved, although not very social. Mr. Healy commented that Susan has displayed appropriate social skills at times, but frequently "she becomes so obsessed about a particular topic that other children shy away from her." Mr. Healy noted that Susan does well academically but often has difficulty when taking tests that tap reflective thought. Mr. Healy stated that "Susan often begins to answer the question, but goes into such detail about a small portion of the answer and then seems to forget to focus on answering the entire question."

Perhaps Susan has difficulty shifting her mental set from the details to the gestalt of the test item. Mr. Healy modified Susan's tests so that each question included "In your answer please address . . ." and then he numbered the various points he wanted her to write about on her paper. This testing format allowed Susan to benefit from the structure of the question, without giving her the answers, and thus maintained the usefulness of the test as a measure of her knowledge.

Individuals with a "reduced ability to automatically and unconsciously disattend selectively to their own intrusive thoughts may . . . be vulnerable to developing OCD" (Clayton, Richards, & Edwards, 1999, p. 174). Clayton and colleagues (1999) note that children with OCD have difficulty shifting focus from their preoccupation and may, therefore, appear to have an attention deficit. In other words, these youngsters may continue to focus on the preoccupation rather than on the topic or activity that others ask them to engage in at a particular time. Given this information, teachers should consider the possibility that a child who presents with inattention may be internally preoccupied and suffering from OCD, although other explanations, such as ADHD, depression, or a host of other disorders or concerns may more easily account for the overt distractibility in a particular student.

Suggestions for Teachers: Helping OCD Children in the Classroom

Swedo and Rapoport (1989) note that it is important to "remember that OCD is an illness" (p. 149). I have spoken with numerous children who have had OCD symptoms. Many of them (although not all) benefited from knowing that the teacher was aware of the problem, respected them as individuals, but would also try to assist them in participating in school activities rather than fixating on the OCD symptoms. At times, a child's therapist and teacher can communicate to develop a school-based intervention strategy.

POSSIBLE INTERVENTION STRATEGIES

- Gradually increase expectations for the child's focus and participation in classroom work.
- Ask the child to rate his or her subjective experiences of stress and distress during the day so that connections can be made between events and symptoms.

- Allow the child to tell the teacher when the obsessions or compulsions are interfering with concentration so that the child does not feel isolated and alone or otherwise out of place.
- Establish contact with the school-based team of specialists (and/or the child's therapist) in order to develop a multidisciplinary approach to helping the student.

An appropriate intervention plan needs to be tailored not only to the OCD symptoms that are present but also to the child's personality, the environment that the student is placed in, the family's support of the intervention, and the availability of support staff (e.g., school psychologist) to assist in implementing the particular plan.

LISA AND EVAN: SUFFERING FROM OCD?

Let us now return to our two case examples, Lisa and Evan. In earlier sections of this book, I have stated that each of their behavioral presentations could be accounted for by a number of different factors. Could they each be suffering from an obsessive–compulsive disorder? Since some of the overt symptoms may not be evident in school, the teacher may not notice any compulsions for Lisa. Perhaps she only experiences obsessions, such as a preoccupation with concerns about her health or safety. Her withdrawn behavior may reflect her inattention to the classroom environment because she is predominantly attending to her internal thoughts. For Evan, his frequent trips to the bathroom may be due to a compulsion, such as a need to frequently wash his hands.

It is easy to fit some of Lisa's and Evan's symptoms into this broad category, but it is difficult to determine whether it is a *good* fit. Interventions are developed based on an accurate diagnosis, so a concerned teacher should consider speaking with Lisa's or Evan's parent to gather more information and then consulting with the school counselor to determine whether OCD is a potential cause for the behaviors or symptoms.

PERFECTIONISM

As the illustrations at the beginning of this chapter highlighted, personality characteristics can be adaptive for one individual (e.g., intense focus) while being dysfunctional for another (e.g., an irrational obsession). Perfectionistic strivings can also fall into these two categories. Certainly, teachers and parents have asked children to try their best in all that they do. For Jack, a socially popular second-grade student who generally worked hard to complete tasks and took pride in his accomplishments, his high goals neither hampered his ability to function nor negatively affected his self-esteem. He was able to laugh at his mistakes, learn from his errors, and work to improve himself. Unfortunately, some youngsters can become disabled by their perfectionistic standards.

RAYMOND: OBSESSED WITH PERFECTION

Eleven-year-old Raymond developed an obsession about the need to be perfect. He despised writing because he never felt that his letters were formed well, he never thought that his ideas were expressed clearly enough, and he frequently erased his words to improve on his work. When Raymond would look at his paper, filled with remnants of eraser marks, he would become upset that the paper no longer looked "nice." Over time, Raymond began to display oppositional behaviors when his teacher asked him to begin a writing task. He refused to begin the work so that he could avoid producing a less-than-perfect product. Raymond also avoided participating in all sports because he felt that he might make mistakes. For Raymond, his high standards led to a decrease in productivity and lower self-esteem, since he felt that he could never fulfill his own perfectionistic expectations.

Flett, Hewitt, Blankstein, and Gray (1998) note that perfectionists often focus on reaching idealized standards rather than on reaching more realistic, attainable goals. There are many reasons why a child may become perfectionistic. I have had the experience of working with abused children who are fearful of doing anything wrong and disappointing the abusive adult. One could argue about whether such students are truly perfectionistic or simply realistically anticipating severe consequences for imperfect actions. Other children may be perfectionistic because of numerous other reasons, such as an attempt to compete with older siblings, a view of things as all good or all bad, OCD symptoms, a fear of taking risks and failing, or low self-esteem.

Hewitt, Flett, Ediger, Norton, and Flynn (1998) described three types of perfectionism:

Self-oriented perfectionism is an intraindividual component that involves requiring the self to be perfect. Socially prescribed perfectionism is an interpersonal dimension that involves the need to meet the perceived perfectionistic expectations that others place on an individual; other-oriented perfectionism involves requiring perfection of others. (p. 235)

Striving to excel is a positive characteristic, yet when taken to the point of perfectionism, it has been associated with mood disorders such as depression (e.g., Flett et al., 1998; Hewitt et al., 1998) and anxiety (e.g., Flett et al., 1998). Therefore, teachers who become aware of a student who sets

:ally high expectations, or does not enjoy the journey of learning
_f a fear of not being perfect in the learning process), should consider the fact that perfectionism may be hampering the child's functioning and emotional well-being.

To return to our case examples, Lisa and Evan, it is possible that Lisa withdraws rather than risk failure and Evan escapes (e.g., leaves the room, distracts himself from work) for similar reasons. Despite the desire to be perfect, some perfectionists actually produce less, withdraw more, and appear to be apathetic and unmotivated. This style can allow them to believe that they could have been perfect if they had tried rather than have to admit that they tried but failed to attain their unrealistically high standards.

*ALL CHILDREN, ESPECIALLY PERFECTIONISTS,
SHOULD KNOW THE FOLLOWING:*

- Mistakes can result in opportunities to learn and grow.
- Taking on a new task and trying hard is something in which to take pride.
- Accepting the challenge of being an imperfect human being can relieve some personal pressure to always be perfect.
- People can be imperfect yet enjoy themselves and their lives.

DEPRESSION

"It is now widely accepted that Major Depressive Disorder (MDD) exists among children and adolescents" (Craighead, Smucker, Craighead, & Ilardi, 1998, p. 156). Depression is an area of particular concern for many teachers who seek to identify children at risk of self-injurious behaviors. Although not all depressed children are suicidal, symptoms of depression are important to review since they can significantly impact a student's life.

Perhaps two illustrations will help to highlight some of the ways in which a child can display and experience depression.

**VICTOR AND TARA:
TWO DIFFERENT PRESENTATIONS OF DEPRESSION**

Mrs. Davis, Victor's third-grade teacher, met with the school principal about her concerns regarding Victor's behaviors and attitude. She reported that Victor often informed his classmates that he thinks school is "awful" and that the assignments "don't matter." Victor had few friends and was in detention frequently for fighting on the playground or for throwing pieces of his food at children as they passed him in the cafeteria.

Mrs. Davis did not feel that the work was unmanageable for Victor; she thought he attained low grades because of lack of effort. When questioned about his apparent lack of interest in school, Victor would shrug his shoulders and not express any motivation to communicate his feelings or to work harder.

The principal suggested that Mrs. Davis speak with Victor's mother and perhaps with the school psychologist, since consequences and disciplinary actions had been ineffective in helping Victor. Mrs. Davis spoke with Victor's mother and learned that Victor often complained of being "bored" at home, had difficulty sleeping, and rarely played with any of his peers. After consent was obtained, the school psychologist talked directly with Victor. Victor initially refused to talk, other than to report that he hated school and viewed most things as "boring." Upon further investigation, however, Victor admitted that he frequently felt inadequate, believed that no one liked him, and stayed up at night thinking about how disappointed his parents must be to have him as their son. After a thorough mental health assessment, which included parent and teacher input as well as a psychiatric consultation, Victor was diagnosed with depression.

Tara presented in a very different manner from Victor, yet she, too, was later diagnosed with depression. Tara's father contacted Tara's teacher to ask for assistance because he was no longer sure what to do to help his daughter. He stated that Tara often cried and never took pride in her accomplishments. She was perfectionistic and always seemed to disappoint herself in any task she undertook. Despite the fact that Tara had several close friends and family members, was of average weight, and was typically described as "cute," Tara commented that she was ugly, fat, hated by her classmates, and unlovable. At times, Tara scared her father by stating, "I might as well just kill myself." Tara's father and teacher both agreed that Tara expected herself to fail and disappoint others, that she had recently displayed increased distractibility, and that she no longer engaged in some of her favorite activities (e.g., dancing). After receiving a private psychiatric evaluation, Tara was diagnosed with a major depressive disorder and began treatment.

Defining Depression and Dysthymic Disorder

The American Psychiatric Association (2000) states that a major depressive disorder may be present when a child displays a depressed or irritable mood or when a person exhibits decreased interest in things or activities that formally were viewed positively. Other symptoms, according to the American Psychiatric Association (2000), can include weight loss (or, for a child, failure to gain weight, as expected, over time) and changes in sleep, as well as

> psychomotor agitation or retardation, . . . feeling of worthlessness or excessive or inappropriate guilt . . . nearly every day, . . . diminished ability to think or concentrate, or indecisiveness, nearly every day . . . recurrent thoughts of death . . . [and] recurrent suicidal ideation. . . . (p. 356)

It should be noted that a person does not need to exhibit all of the symptoms to be diagnosed with depression. However, the American Psychiatric

Association (2000) indicates that the symptoms must involve significant "distress or impairment" in functioning (p. 356).

Dysthymic disorder is also a depressive disorder, differing from a major depressive disorder on several factors, such as "duration, persistence, and severity" of symptoms (APA, 2000, p. 379). "Dysthymic Disorder is characterized by chronic, less severe depressive symptoms" than those of a major depressive disorder (APA, 2000, p. 379). However, Cicchetti and Toth (1998) note that dysthymia "is one of the major pathways to recurrent depressive disorder" (p. 223).

There are many ways in which a child can display symptoms of, or experience, depression and dysthymia. Poland (1989) states that the following symptoms may be evident in depressed children and adolescents:

> Withdrawal from friends and activities; loss of joy in life and a bleak outlook for the future; changes in sleeping and eating habits; risk-taking or reckless behavior; preoccupation with death; increased somatic complaints; concentration problems with regard to school work; frequent mood changes; uncharacteristic emotional or rebellious outbursts; low self-esteem and lack of confidence in abilities and decision-making capabilities; significant weight loss or gain; [and] decreased attention to physical appearance. (p. 36)

The Research

Although the incidence of major depressive disorder may be similar in boys and girls (Cicchetti & Toth, 1998), the manifestation of symptoms may vary somewhat along gender lines. For instance, Craighead and colleagues (1998) found that, on the Children's Depression Inventory, boys were more likely to score high on characteristics such as "misbehavior, disobedience, and aggression . . . drop in school performance . . . social withdrawal . . . school dislike and anhedonia" (p. 158). Girls scored higher on characteristics that involved "sadness, crying spells, irritability, and loneliness . . . self-hate, negative body image, low self-esteem, and feeling unloved" (p. 158).

McGrath and Repetti (2002) report that youngsters who have symptoms of depression tend to feel more negatively about themselves and about their social as well as academic abilities than do other children. Despite the significant ramifications of depression on a child's views of his or her life functioning, research suggests that adults around them may not be aware of the severity of the symptoms that children subjectively experience (e.g., Epkins, 1996). McClure, Kubiszyn, and Kaslow (2002) reviewed the literature and found that adults may be able to identify behaviorally observable symptoms of depressive states in children, but youngsters themselves can also help a diagnostician determine whether depression is present. The children may be able to describe their emotional concerns and possible suicidal thoughts. Therefore, it may be helpful for teachers to gently invite students to share their feelings and self-perceptions if there is a concern about possible low self-esteem or depression.

Depression is a multidimensional disorder that often affects mood, behavior, social relationships, and so on. Cicchetti and Toth (1998) comment that depression involves the "interplay of psychological (e.g., affective, cognitive, socioemotional, social-cognitive), social (e.g., community, culture), and biological (e.g., genetic, neurobiological, . . . neurochemical, neuroendocrine) components" (p. 224).

In regard to the physiological aspects of depression, a child is at increased risk of developing the disorder if there is a family history (APA, 2000). Another indication that there may be a physiological factor in depression was reported in a study conducted by Kentgen and colleagues (2000). They reviewed electroencephalogram (EEG) findings on a group of female adolescents who were noted to be clinically depressed and found "abnormal EEG alpha patterns" (p. 801). The authors assert that their results show a relationship between major depression in teenagers and an "alpha asymmetry at posterior sites" of the brain (p. 801). It is unclear whether adolescent physiological correlates of depression can be generalized to children with this disorder.

LISA AND EVAN: DEPRESSED?

Let us return to our two case examples, Lisa and Evan, to determine whether they might each be suffering from depression. Lisa displays social withdrawal and lack of energy. These can be two symptoms of depression. Evan displays agitation and irritability. Evan's symptoms can also reflect underlying depression, despite the fact that his overt symptoms are quite different from those displayed by Lisa. Just by looking at each of these children, it would be extremely difficult to determine whether they are depressed, anxious, learning disabled (and feeling that school is too difficult), or suffering from another disorder.

Understanding Suicidal Ideation

Suicidal ideation (thoughts) is a topic that warrants some discussion in this section, since the potential consequences are lethal. First, it is important to note that youngsters may verbalize suicidal thoughts for a variety of reasons.

JASON: SUICIDAL?

Twelve-year-old Jason, for example, threatened suicide each time he got in trouble, since he knew that his teacher and parents would become concerned and give him positive attention rather than punish him. Jason was manipulative, but his manipulation still required exploration—his particular form of manipulation must have been chosen (consciously or unconsciously) for a reason. In other words, it would be helpful to understand the reason Jason adopted this strategy of manipulation. For instance, was he acting defiant in this manner as part of a conduct disorder, struggling with impulsivity, or talking about suicide because of other factors that need to be assessed (e.g., his desire for more attention from important others in his life).

Not Depressed, but They Kill Themselves? Some children may actually kill themselves, despite the fact that they are not clinically depressed. For instance, if a 2-year-old jumps out of a window in a high-rise building to be able to fly with the birds, this unfortunate death may be due to lack of judgment rather than lack of desire to live. In addition, a youngster who ends his or her life as a result of a command hallucination (a psychotic state where the child hears a voice within his or her own head demanding a particular action) and a preadolescent who recklessly dies because of poor judgment as he or she followed up on a dare proposed by peers present quite different characteristics from that of the depressed child who commits suicide.

Self-Mutilating Behavior. There are also some people who purposely harm themselves but deny suicidal intent. For instance, an adolescent who is a self-mutilator may not be suicidal but may engage in "low lethality, socially unacceptable self-injury . . . such as skin cutting [and] self-inflicted burns" (Haines, Williams, Brain, & Wilson, 1995, p. 471). Haines and colleagues (1995) propose that individuals engage in such actions because of "the rewarding tension reducing qualities of the self-mutilative act [that serves to] reinforce and maintain the behavior as an effective, although maladaptive, coping strategy" (p. 488). In my professional experience, the self-mutilator's tension is frequently the result of anger that cannot be expressed externally and is, therefore, turned against him- or herself.

ABRAHAM: SUICIDE AS AN ESCAPE

Depressed students may subjectively view suicide as a viable solution for escaping the emotional pain, especially if the youngster feels hopeless and helpless in life. This was the case for 11-year-old Abraham. Abraham felt that he never gained acceptance in his new school when he moved there at the beginning of the academic year. In the four months since he became a student at this school, Abraham was painfully aware that he had not had a single playdate, a phone call from a classmate, or an invitation to a party. The reason for his move was because his parents divorced, his mother remarried, and she bought a house with Abraham's stepfather. Abraham felt alienated from his father, angry at his mother for moving, and unloved by his new stepfather. He felt that no one liked being around him and that his future would only bring further pain. Academically, Abraham believed that he could not excel, so "why bother trying to do the work?"

In early January, Abraham and another student, Max, were outside during recess and began to argue with each other. Max said "Drop dead!" to Abraham, who then responded by saying, "Don't worry, I intend to!" before stomping off. During the next week, Abraham's teacher noticed that he finally seemed to be less angry, less agitated, and less challenging of class rules. His teacher viewed this as a sign of progress.

Fortunately, Max eventually talked to his father about the altercation that had occurred during recess the prior week, because he had been concerned about Abraham's comment. Max's father phoned the school principal and reported the incident. After the school principal and school psychologist investigated the comment, by talking with Abraham, speaking with his teacher, gathering information from both of his biological parents and from his stepfather, and looking at the pattern of Abraham's functioning over time, it was determined that Abraham was a suicide risk.

In fact, Abraham's behavior appeared to improve at the exact time that he determined that he would kill himself. He felt comfortable with this decision. He believed that he would soon be reunited with his deceased aunt in the wonderful place that he pictured heaven to be. He had suicidal ideation (thought), he intended to kill himself, and he had a plan. Abraham had taken much of the liquid medication from the family's medicine cabinet and planned to mix it all together into a deadly drink.

Abraham was immediately seen by a child psychiatrist to determine whether medication or hospitalization was indicated. The psychiatrist felt that Abraham would benefit from an antidepressant medication, short-term hospitalization until the crisis period ended and the medication began to take effect, and then intensive outpatient therapy. The doctor noted that Abraham seemed to be relieved that others cared about his emotional distress and that Abraham appeared to be willing to see whether interventions might help.

With intensive therapy, which included individual and family work, as well as close communication between Abraham's therapist and teacher, Abraham began to become more hopeful about his future and less depressed. He eventually realized that his biological parents had not meant to reject him and that they did not respond to his feelings of being overwhelmed and depressed because they were unaware of how hurt, angry, and depressed he had been. He began to spend more time with his stepfather and found that they had some similar interests. Eventually, Abraham entered into a social skills group to help him to develop skills that would foster more positive peer interactions.

If Max had not reported Abraham's brief comment, if Max's father had not taken it seriously and reported it to the school, and if the school had not responded, the consequences could have been devastating. For this reason, Poland (1989) states that "every reference to suicide should warn teachers to inquire further and to consider referral through the proper channels at school" (p. 43). I would add that *all* comments about harming oneself or others, and signs of depression, should be reported to the appropriate school personnel (e.g., school psychologist, school social worker, consulting psychiatrist) so that the teacher can be a part of a team effort to prevent tragedies such as suicide or homicide.

Risk Factors for Suicide. There are no cookbook criteria to determine whether a child is serious about a suicidal threat. Therefore, it is important to take all statements seriously until they can be further investigated. However, research has shown that some factors are more typical of suicidal individuals. For instance, Pfeffer, Jiang, and Kakuma (2000) reviewed the literature and state:

> Empirical research suggests that risk factors for youth suicidal behavior can be classified as (a) psychiatric symptoms and psychiatric disorders, especially impulsivity, mood, anxiety, disruptive behavior, substance abuse, and personality disorders . . . (b) family discord and psychopathology, including violence, depression, substance abuse, and personality disorders . . . (c) stressful experiences, particularly abuse and losses of emotionally important people . . . and (d) cognitive factors involving competence in academic and social activities and perceptions of hopelessness. (p. 304)

Sternberg and colleagues (1993) assessed 110 children between the ages of 8 and 12 and concluded that those who had been victims of child abuse and those who had "both witnessed and been physically abused . . . were more likely than children in the comparison group to report depressive symptoms" (p. 49). In a study assessing suicidal thoughts, Kashani, Reid, and Rosenberg (1989) found that "in the no-hopelessness group there were no suicidal children and that in only 4% of the moderate-hopelessness group was there recurrent suicidal ideation. In contrast, one third (33.3%) of the high-hopelessness group had recurrent suicidal ideation" (pp. 498–499). This information illustrates how a child's sense of control is inversely related to depressive symptoms and suicidal ideation.

Poland (1989) reports that some individuals are at increased risk of suicide during certain periods of the year. This can be referred to as an anniversary reaction—for instance, the anniversary of a parent's death or other significant event.

Suggestions for Teachers: Be Alert to Warning Signs

Poland (1989) also offers a suggestion to teachers as they attempt to help students in their classrooms. He notes that it is important to "pay attention to the content of student themes, poems, and artwork" (p. 2). Sometimes a student may express feelings in writing rather than ask to speak with the teacher about the concern.

Periodically, children may confide in a teacher about suicidal thoughts, but then ask the teacher to keep the secret and not tell others. It is an awkward position for any teacher to have to break a confidence, but I have found that many children can eventually understand that the teacher talked with other adults about the suicidal thoughts as a way to seek assistance to better help them. Once the child's physical well-being is protected, the teacher can then talk with the young student about who will need to know the information and what might occur (e.g., a meeting with the school psychologist; parent–principal meeting, and then a referral to another mental health professional).

In class, it is important to help all children feel hopeful, capable, socially connected, and academically competent. However, it may not be possible to reach every student on each level. Therefore, the teacher should always be alert for those children who may be experiencing depression or suicidal thoughts.

The mental health professional who evaluates a child for depression or suicide potential will look at numerous factors. McClure and colleagues (2002) wrote about the evaluation process involved in assessing a child for depression. They note that "assessments of the prepubertal child should be comprehensive and include collection of family, medical, developmental, attachment, psychosocial, and presenting problem histories from multiple informants" (p. 131). The mental health evaluator will also need to hear the child's perspective on his or her life and determine whether that child is clinically depressed or may be suffering from another challenge or disorder.

Other Disorders of Mood

Depression is considered to be a disorder of mood. There are numerous other disorders in this category, including bipolar disorders. A person with a bipolar disorder may display manic or manic-like behaviors, possibly along with periods of depression. The American Psychiatric Association (2000) includes in its list of characteristics seen in individuals suffering from a "manic episode" the following: "inflated self-esteem or grandiosity; decreased need for sleep; more talkative than usual or pressure to keep talking; flight of ideas or subjective experience that thoughts are racing; [and] distractibility" (p. 362). The symptoms must impair important areas of functioning if they are to be diagnostically significant for the determination of the presence of this disorder.

Bipolar disorders have overlapping characteristics with other diagnoses and concerns (e.g., attention-deficit hyperactivity disorder; agitated anxiety; some side effects of medication or physical problems), so a careful evaluation is essential to determine the accurate disorder. Papolos and Papolos (1999) comment that "it is estimated that one-third of all the children in this country who have been diagnosed with attention-deficit disorder with hyperactivity (ADHD) are actually suffering from early symptoms of bipolar disorder" (p. 4). In regard to children, however, McClure and colleagues (2002) note that "the concept of prepubertal" bipolar disorder "continues to generate controversy" (p. 129).

MIND–BODY INTERACTION: PHYSICAL ILLNESS AND ITS RELATION TO EMOTIONAL STRESS

When a student complains about having a stomachache, feeling nauseous, or having a bad headache, the teacher may question whether the stated symptom is genuine, a way to avoid work, or symbolic of an overwhelming emotional concern. Since the mind and body are integrally connected, answering this question can be difficult and the answer will vary from child to child.

Young children may not have the words to verbalize their emotions, so they might communicate their tension by telling the teacher that "I need to call my mommy; I'm sick" or "I don't feel good, so I need to go to the nurse." For such students, quick lessons on more precise ways to communicate anxiety, anger, sadness, or frustration may be quite effective. I have found that even kindergarten children can easily begin to report that "I miss my mommy; I need to call her" or "I feel nervous because I can't do the math." Once the statements accurately reflect the student's concern, then the teacher can respond more directly.

Some students will report somatic concerns and actually believe that they are ill. The anxious student, for example, may experience sweating, a rapid pulse, or lightheadedness. The physical symptoms may be caused by his or her emotional state. Once medical causes for the physical sensations are ruled out, the child's parent or the school counselor might begin to educate the child about anxiety and the fact that the physical symptoms can be directly related to it. This information may reduce the panic that the child can experience when symptoms emerge. The importance of looking at both the mind and body when determining the reason for anxiety, and having the child (and his or her family) consult with a medical as well as mental health professional is important, since anxiety can lead to physical reactions and physical conditions can lead to anxiety.

This connection between one's feelings and bodily concerns is evident not only in the case of anxiety. Some individuals respond to emotions such as anger, humiliation, and sadness, for example, by experiencing physical discomfort. Likewise, medical difficulties can make a child feel more vulnerable and overwhelmed, which may be manifested in an increase in emotional reactivity. For this reason, it is important to include the school nurse in the investigation of a child's physical complaints.

In their investigation of 540 children from second through twelfth grades, Garber, Walker, and Zeman (1991) found that there can be a connection between emotional concerns and physical complaints. The investigators reported that those youngsters who had a high degree of self-confidence and a low degree of anxious and depressive symptoms were less likely to report somatic complaints than others in the sample.

Shyness and Physical Distress

The connection between the mind and body is highlighted in a report by Chung and Evans (2000). They "investigated the association between shyness and symptoms of illness in young children" of approximately 7 years of age (p. 49). The authors found that "there were more days on which shy children complained of unwellness and parents observed symptoms of unwellness than for nonshy children" (p. 49). They also raised questions about whether the stress associated with shyness leads to more somatic complaints, noting that some data presented in other research has shown higher cortisol levels in shy versus control subjects. In addition, these authors speculate that shy children who withdraw from perceived stresses, such as school and playdates, may then experience further tension later when exposed to these events.

I have professionally encountered numerous shy children who seek to avoid uncomfortable situations, feel immediately relieved when avoidance is accomplished, but then become more uncomfortable when later asked to encounter the same event. The avoidance not only keeps shy children from gaining the confidence to master the stress; it also may keep them from modeling others and learning ways to interact in the particular environment. This pattern may also be observed in young students who avoid social situations due to social anxiety.

Chronic Illness and Subjective Stress

There are times when a child has a documented medical condition, such as diabetes or asthma. Even in these cases, however, the young person's emotions and levels of subjective stress can impact physical difficulties. Diabetes mellitus, for the purpose of this discussion, will be described as a disease that

> develops when the pancreas is unable to produce an adequate supply of insulin, a hormone needed to metabolize glucose . . . [and the] goal of treatment is to regulate the balance between insulin and glucose in the bloodstream to avoid such . . . complications as hypoglycemia and hyperglycemia . . . neuropathy, heart and kidney disease. (Martin, Miller-Johnson, Kitzmann, & Emery, 1998, p. 102)

Feifer and Tansman (1999) reviewed the literature on diabetes and report that "psychiatric disorders, such as depression, can create a disruption in the internal metabolic control of people with diabetes as well as with their self-care routine" (p. 18) and that it is important not to "overlook psychological disorders' interaction with compliance and complications" (p. 17). Therefore, when a person suffers from a medical condition, the possibility that emotions and stress may impact the disease and can also influence one's treatment follow-up should be considered.

Asthma is "a chronic respiratory disease" (Lehrer, Feldman, Giardino, Song, & Schmaling, 2002, p. 691) that has been studied extensively. This disease can be reactive to the interaction among one's emotions, environment, and physiology. For instance, during an allergy-induced asthmatic attack, it is not unusual for a child to experience severe emotional stress. Lehrer and colleagues (2002) note:

> There is no solid evidence indicating that behavioral factors *cause* asthma . . . [but] there is evidence that certain negative emotions, particularly panic and depression, even when not severe enough to be classifiable as a psychiatric disorder, may produce respiratory effects that are consistent with exacerbation of asthma . . . [emotions can have] effects on asthma self-care . . . [and have] direct psychophysiological effects on the lung. . . . [In addition,] emotional states can be triggered by asthma. (p. 703, emphasis in original)

Each student in a classroom may react uniquely to academic tasks, environmental stimuli (e.g., allergens), amount of sleep obtained the previous night, type of food eaten, subjective stress of one's social world and family situation, interactions with the teacher, and physiological factors. Teachers should be comforted by knowing that they cannot be an expert in *all* areas and, thus, might want to seek the professional input of those in the building who are specialists in the various areas (e.g., principal, school nurse, school physician, school psychologist) and consult with the child's parent and even the child's treating physician, if appropriate.

The Impact of Chronic Medical Concerns

Fatigue. During the school careers of most youngsters, they will have brief absences from school due to relatively minor medical illnesses. For the chronically ill child, though, there are some unique school-related challenges. For instance, a child who is fatigued following a round of chemotherapy or a child who is in chronic pain from sickle-cell anemia or following a car accident may find it difficult to focus on academic tasks.

Cognitive and Emotional Impact. Medical problems sometimes impact a student's cognitive and emotional state. Holmes, O'Brien, and Greer (1995), for instance, report that "studies with diabetic children . . . found decreases in decision-making efficiency and attention during hypoglycemia" (p. 331). Freeman (1979) states that there is "evidence that children with epilepsy experience a high incidence of learning disabilities" (p. 172); more recently, Black and Hynd (1995) also reported that "learning problems in particular seem to occur in children with epilepsy" (p. 349). Other medical difficulties, such as malnutrition (Wachs et al., 1995), significant lead poisoning, and HIV-related factors (Wolters, Brouwers, & Moss, 1995) may also have an impact on a child's school performance.

BETTY: LAZY OR MEDICALLY ILL?

At times a teacher may be concerned about a child yet have no obvious reason to suspect that the difficulty is due to an underlying physical problem. Betty, for example, was described as being "lazy, unmotivated, and maybe a little depressed" by her teacher. She was later diagnosed as suffering from petit mal seizures, which are brief lapses of consciousness that may lead an observer to thinking the individual is simply daydreaming. Medication was instituted and improvements were noted. Since most school personnel, with the exception of the school nurse and physician, often have limited if any medical training, teachers should encourage parents to inform the pediatrician of any academic, social, emotional, or behavioral concerns regarding their children. Although symptoms similar to those displayed by Betty are often not due to medical causes, the doctor can determine whether, in a particular situation, medical evaluations are necessary.

Impact of Certain Medications. Medications used to treat physical illnesses can also affect a student's school performance, such as by decreasing concentration abilities or altering one's energy level. As a school psychologist, I have witnessed children responding in a variety of ways to medications. For example, Jody became extremely lethargic, while Marshall became quite restless and disruptive.

If we revisit the case examples of Evan and Lisa, it is possible that Evan and Lisa have both recently started taking medication, leading Evan to become restless and excitable and Lisa to become withdrawn. When the classroom teacher, doctor, and parents communicate about the medications and the potential side effects, then the teacher is in a better position to understand the child's needs and make helpful accommodations for that youngster.

Extended School Absences and School Accommodations. The chronically ill child may miss significant amounts of school because of medical treatment. The doctor, in consultation with the teacher and parents, might be able to offer guidelines regarding how much work the child can handle. A child may experience feelings of satisfaction after completing schoolwork and may have some increased feelings of competence. This individual will also feel less confused regarding academic work upon returning to school if modified assignments (or home schooling) are offered during the medical absence.

When a child is faced with a serious physical illness, it may be hard for that youngster, and for the involved adults, to decide how much support is needed and how much independent action should be encouraged. Some children may refuse any assistance as a way to prove that they are in control; at the other extreme, some children may become quite dependent and feel helpless about their ability to control their lives. Teachers and parents also have to balance their desire to take care of the youngster with their desire to help that student regain self-confidence in his or her ability to function independently. Bain (1995) comments that "when a child experiences a trauma such as that of having cancer, the line between protection and overprotection often becomes blurred" (p. 159).

When a child has been ill and out of school for an extended period of time, a planned reentry might be arranged. In this plan, the parents, teacher, and medical doctor can collaborate to prepare for the occasion. The patient may feel more secure and self-assured about returning to class if given the opportunity to participate in the reentry planning process. Teachers who are kept informed about a child's medical needs (e.g., a diabetic student's need to have snack during class) will be better prepared to handle the changes that a child's illness necessitates.

Peer Responses to the Ill Child. At times, "elementary school aged peers, concerned that the disease is contagious, may shun interaction with the child" (Sexson & Madan-Swain, 1995, p. 362). Therefore, one part of the reentry plan may include having the teacher educate the other students about the ill youngster's difficulties. Educating other students about the student's illness, physical appearance, and needs, either before or after the student returns to school, may help alleviate fears and make the reentry experience more posi-tive for all (Bain, 1995). Some ill youngsters, however, would be uncomfort-able with this plan, perhaps because they prefer a less public acknowledgment of their medical problem; other options may need to be explored in these cases.

Tailoring Interventions to the Particular Student's Needs. A child with a chronic illness may not display the concerns raised above. In fact, some stu-dents may gain new insight into the mind–body interaction, physiology, nutrition, and the amount of emotional strength that was untapped prior to the medical difficulty. Therefore, educators will always need to look at each child as an individual who may respond to the stress of a physical disorder in a wide variety of ways.

Children with medical conditions may also experience learning, emo-tional, or behavioral concerns outlined in other sections of this book. These areas of difficulty may or may not be related to the child's medical prob-lems. Here, again, it can be quite helpful for parents, teachers, and doctors to communicate about major changes in the child's functioning, so that the changes can be assessed and quickly addressed.

It is important, at this point, to remind the reader that the information presented here is specific to children of elementary school age; some of the previously stated recommendations would be somewhat different if the pa-tient were an adolescent, including increased patient responsibility in the treatment process, more direct doctor–patient communication, and fewer parent–teacher discussions that do not include the student.

CONCLUSION

In this chapter, some of the internalized concerns that can affect children in the classroom were discussed. Specifically, obsessive and compulsive symp-toms, along with obsessive–compulsive disorder, were reviewed. In addition, perfectionism, depression, suicidal thoughts and intent, and the interaction of the mind and body were explored. The effects of chronic medical difficul-ties on a student's school functioning were also addressed.

REFERENCES

American Psychiatric Association (APA). (2000). *Diagnostic and statistical manual of mental disorders: Fourth edition, DSM-IV-TR, text revision*. Washington, DC: Author.

Bain, L. J. (1995). *A parent's guide to childhood cancer*. New York: Dell.

Black, K. C., & Hynd, G. W. (1995). Epilepsy in the school aged child: Cognitive-behavioral characteristics and effects on academic performance. *School Psychology Quarterly, 10*(4), 345–358.

Chung, J. Y. Y., & Evans, M. A. (2000). Shyness and symptoms of illness in young children. *Canadian Journal of Behavioural Science, 32*(1), 49–57.

Cicchetti, D., & Toth S. L. (1998). The development of depression in children and adolescents. *American Psychologist, 53*(2), 221–241.

Clayton, I. C., Richards, J. C., & Edwards, C. J. (1999). Selective attention in obsessive-compulsive disorder. *Journal of Abnormal Psychology, 108*(1), 171–175.

Craighead, W. E., Smucker, M. R., Craighead, L. W., & Ilardi, S. S. (1998). Factor analysis of the Children's Depression Inventory in a community sample. *Psychological Assessment, 10*(2), 156–165.

Epkins, C. C. (1996). Parent ratings of children's depression, anxiety, and aggression: A cross-sample analysis of agreement and differences with child and teacher ratings. *Journal of Clinical Psychology, 52*(6), 599–608.

Feifer, C., & Tansman, M. (1999). Promoting psychology in diabetes primary care. *Professional Psychology: Research and Practice, 30*(1), 14–21.

Flett, G. L., Hewitt, P. L., Blankstein, K. R., & Gray, L. (1998). Psychological distress and the frequency of perfectionistic thinking. *Journal of Personality and Social Psychology, 75*(5), 1363–1381.

Franklin, M. E., Abramowitz, J. S., Bux, D. A., Zoellner, L. A., & Feeny, N. C. (2002). Cognitive-behavioral therapy with and without medication in the treatment of obsessive-compulsive disorder. *Professional Psychology: Research and Practice, 33*(2), 162–168.

Freeman, S. W. (1979). *The epileptic in home, school and society*. Springfield, IL: Charles C. Thomas.

Garber, J., Walker, L. S., & Zeman, J. (1991). Somatization symptoms in a community sample of children and adolescents: Further validation of the Children's Somatization Inventory. *Psychological Assessment: A Journal of Consulting and Clinical Psychology, 3*(4), 588–595.

Haines, J., Williams, C. L., Brain, K. L., & Wilson, G. V. (1995). The psychophysiology of self-mutilation. *Journal of Abnormal Psychology, 104*(3), 471–489.

Hanna, G. L. (1995). Demographic and clinical features of obsessive-compulsive disorder in children and adolescents. *Journal of the American Academy of Child and Adolescent Psychiatry, 34*(1), 19–27.

Hewitt, P. L., Flett, G. L., Ediger, E., Norton, G. R., & Flynn, C. A. (1998). Perfectionism in chronic and state symptoms of depression. *Canadian Journal of Behavioural Science, 30*(4), 234–242.

Holmes, C. S., O'Brien, B., & Greer, T. (1995). Cognitive functioning and academic achievement in children with insulin-dependent diabetes mellitus (IDDM). *School Psychology Quarterly, 10*(4), 329–344.

Kashani, J. H., Reid, J. C., & Rosenberg, T. K. (1989). Levels of hopelessness in children and adolescents: A developmental perspective. *Journal of Consulting and Clinical Psychology, 57*(4), 496–499.

Kentgen, L. M., Tenke, C. E., Pine, D. S., Fong, R., Klein, R. G., & Bruder, G. E. (2000). Electroencephalographic asymmetries in adolescents with major depression: Influence of comorbidity with anxiety disorders. *Journal of Abnormal Psychology, 109*(4), 797–802.

Lehrer, P., Feldman, J., Giardino, N., Song, H. S., & Schmaling, K. (2002). Psychological aspects of asthma. *Journal of Consulting and Clinical Psychology, 70*(3), 691–711.

Leonard, H. L., Swedo, S. E., Rapoport, J. L., Koby, E. V., Lenane, M. C., Cheslow, D. L., & Hamburger, S. D. (1989). Treatment of obsessive-compulsive disorder with clomipramine and desipramine in children and adolescents. *Archives of General Psychiatry, 46,* 1088–1092.

Martin, M. T., Miller-Johnson, S., Kitzmann, K. M., & Emery, R. E. (1998). Parent–child relationships and insulin-dependent diabetes mellitus: Observational ratings of clinically relevant dimensions. *Journal of Family Psychology, 12*(1), 102–111.

McClure, E. B., Kubiszyn, T., & Kaslow, N. J. (2002). Advances in the diagnosis and treatment of childhood mood disorders. *Professional Psychology: Research and Practice, 33*(2), 125–134.

McGrath, E. P., & Repetti, R. L. (2002). A longitudinal study of children's depressive symptoms, self-perceptions, and cognitive distortions about the self. *Journal of Abnormal Psychology, 111*(1), 77–87.

Papolos, D., & Papolos, J. (1999). *The bipolar child.* New York: Broadway Books.

Pfeffer, C. R., Jiang, H., & Kakuma, T. (2000). Child–Adolescent Suicidal Potential Index (CASPI): A screen for risk for early onset suicidal behavior. *Psychological Assessment, 12*(3), 304–318.

Poland, S. (1989). *Suicide intervention in the schools.* New York: Guilford.

Rapoport, J. L., Leonard, H. L., Swedo, S. E., & Lenane, M. C. (1993). Obsessive compulsive disorder in children and adolescents: Issues in management. *Journal of Clinical Psychiatry, 54*(6), 27–29.

Savage, C. R., Deckersbach, T., Wilhelm, S., Rauch, S. L., Baer, L., Reid, T., & Jenike, M. A. (2000). Strategic processing and episodic memory impairment in obsessive compulsive disorder. *Neuropsychology, 14*(1), 141–151.

Sexson, S., & Madan-Swain, A. (1995). The chronically ill child in the school. *School Psychology Quarterly, 10*(4), 359–368.

Sternberg, K. J., Lamb, M. E., Greenbaum, C., Cicchetti, D., Dawud, S., Cortes, R. M., Krispin, O., & Lorey, F. (1993). Effects of domestic violence on children's behavior problems and depression. *Developmental Psychology, 29*(1), 44–52.

Swedo, S., & Rapoport, J. L. (1989, September). Bad news and good news about obsessive-compulsive disorder. *Contemporary Pediatrics,* pp. 130–151.

Wachs, T. D., Bishry, Z., Moussa, W., Yunis, F., McCabe, G., Harrison, G., Sweifi, E., Kirksey, A., Galal, O., Jerome, N., & Shaheen, F. (1995). Nutritional intake and context as predictors of cognition and adaptive behaviour of Egyptian school-age children. *International Journal of Behavioral Development, 18*(3), 425–450.

Wolters, P. L., Brouwers, P., & Moss, H. A. (1995). Pediatric HIV disease: Effect on cognition, learning, and behavior. *School Psychology Quarterly, 10*(4), 305–328.

CHAPTER 6

Externalized Disorders

ADHD; Oppositional Defiant Disorder; Conduct Disorder and Bullying

This chapter explores externalized disorders, specifically disorders that involve behavioral symptoms. Since children often communicate concerns and feelings through their behaviors, many of the children described in this chapter also have some symptoms of internalized disorders.

ATTENTION-DEFICIT HYPERACTIVITY DISORDER (ADHD)

MARTIN: UNUSUALLY ACTIVE

Martin entered second grade with the same enthusiasm he displayed at the start of each year. However, within a few weeks, he told his mother that "my teacher hates me. She never lets me talk, she never lets me answer questions, and she makes us sit at our desks forever!" Martin's mother had three children, with Martin being the middle child and the only boy. She realized that Martin was quite active, as he often grabbed things out of his sisters' hands, he had difficulty letting others take their turns during board games, and he frequently found excuses to leave the dinner table several times during a single meal.

Martin's mother decided to call her son's teacher, Mrs. Williams, to see if she had similar observations and concerns. In a parent–teacher conference, Mrs. Williams acknowledged that Martin was more active than typical children, that he often rushed through work and seemed to be impatient. He was always playing with something, was restless, frequently paced around the room, and had difficulty sitting during lessons. Typically, Martin blurted out answers during group lessons. When he raised his hand, Mrs. Williams tried to reinforce this effort by calling on him. Mrs. Williams also reported that Martin's high energy and impulsive style appeared to be negatively affecting his peer interactions. However, Mrs. Williams offered Martin's mother some encouragement when she commented that Martin was a bright child who could grasp concepts if he could stay in one place long enough to be taught the material.

Following this meeting, Martin's mother consulted the family pediatrician. He recommended that her son be assessed at a local mental health clinic to determine whether he was suffering from agitated depression, anxiety, boredom due to gifted-ness, an attention-deficit hyperactivity disorder, or some other concern. Martin was evaluated and then diagnosed with an attention-deficit hyperactivity disorder and associated social, school, and family difficulties. He was placed on a psychostimulant medication and received counseling weekly, which focused on his self-esteem issues and self-perceptions as well as helping him to reflect on his approach to academic and social situations. Over time, Martin's mood and level of functioning improved.

CLAUDE: UNMOTIVATED?

Ten-year-old Claude also struggled in school and at home. The school psychologist met with Claude's teacher and then with his mother. According to his mother, Claude is always "in a world of his own," "tunes out whenever he feels like it," and lacks both motivation and perseverance. Claude was described as a youngster who "likes to take the easy way" and often appears to be lethargic despite sleeping well. He can some-times be very attentive when watching television. Claude's teacher reported that he focuses on nonacademic information (e.g., people talking in the hallway) but does not turn the same attention to his work. Claude's mother informed the school psy-chologist that Claude receives time-outs and other consequences for not completing his responsibilities (e.g., loss of television time if he does not finish his homework), yet his behavior has not shown any improvement and he continues to appear unmo-tivated to do anything other than "whatever he wants, like playing on his computer or watching TV." After a thorough assessment by the school counselor and by a medi-cal professional—where anxiety, depression, petit mal seizures, and other conditions were ruled out as the primary concern—Claude was diagnosed with an attention-deficit hyperactivity disorder with associated depressive features.

Defining ADHD

Children who are diagnosed as having an attention-deficit hyperactivity dis-order (ADHD) can manifest symptoms in a variety of ways. For instance, Martin was classified with *ADHD, predominantly hyperactive-impulsive type*. Claude, on the other hand, met the criteria for *ADHD, predominantly inattentive type*. There are other children who have symptoms of both sub-categories and, thus, are diagnosed with *ADHD, combined type*. These three ADHD classifications have been noted by the American Psychiatric Asso-ciation (2000).

An attention-deficit hyperactivity disorder can include symptoms of inattention. To meet the criteria for the predominantly inattentive type of ADHD, the American Psychiatric Association (2000) reports that a person would display many of the following symptoms for a period of at least six months: lacks "attention to details or makes careless mistakes," shows defi-cits in "sustaining attention," "often does not seem to listen when spoken to

directly," tends to lack the perseverance to complete tasks, displays organizational difficulties, "avoids, dislikes or is reluctant to engage in tasks that
require sustained mental effort," misplaces items, is "easily distracted by
extraneous stimuli," and can be described as "forgetful" (p. 92). Claude
exhibited most of these characteristics.

The American Psychiatric Association (2000) notes that a child would
display many of the following symptoms, for a minimum period of six
months, to be diagnosed with the predominantly hyperactive-impulsive type
of ADHD: "fidgets" or "squirms," has difficulty remaining seated to complete tasks, moves about in a way that is inappropriate for one's age, "often
has difficulty playing or engaging in leisure activities quietly," "is often 'on
the go' or often acts as if 'driven by a motor,' often talks excessively," can
interrupt others or "blurt out" comments, and has difficulty with taking
turns (p. 92). Martin displayed many of these characteristics.

The Research

ADHD has been "extensively studied . . . [and] is one of the most commonly
diagnosed childhood disorders" (Aman, Roberts, & Pennington, 1998,
p. 956). According to the literature, this disorder is more common in boys
than in girls (American Psychiatric Association [APA], 2000; Barkley, 1997;
Nigg, 2001; Slone, Durrheim, & Kaminer, 1996). The American Psychiatric Association (2000) and Barkley (1997) report that the incidence of this
disorder is between 3 and 7 percent. ADHD symptoms may persist into adult-
hood in 50 to 65 percent of cases (Barkley, 2000), and ADHD occurs across
cultures (APA, 2000; Slone et al., 1996). Slone and colleagues (1996) state
that "the worldwide and cross-cultural nature of ADHD has been widely
recognized," although occurrence rate "variations . . . have been documented
for the United Kingdom, China, Hong Kong, Canada, and other countries
and for urban versus rural populations" (p. 200).

Diagnosing ADHD

The symptoms of an attention-deficit hyperactivity disorder can easily describe many preschool-aged children. How many 3-year-olds, for instance,
are constantly moving around, have little patience, are restless, and have
difficulty sustaining attention to tasks that are not intrinsically reinforcing?
Many parents report that these symptoms describe their youngsters. However, as a child matures, the expectations to be able to sit still and complete
tasks, to wait to take turns in a game, and so forth, increase. If a child is not
able to display age-appropriate abilities in these areas, then the possibility
that ADHD is hampering functioning may need to be considered. According

to the American Psychiatric Association (2000), some symptoms must begin prior to age 7, although the diagnosis may not be made until later. For instance, if a 9-year-old is being assessed for ADHD, the evaluator would need to conduct a retrospective history to determine whether some of the symptoms of inattention, impulsivity, or hyperactivity were evident before age 7.

LISA AND EVAN: COULD THEY HAVE ADHD?

Let us return to the case examples of Lisa and Evan to determine if either, or both, of them meet the criteria for ADHD. Lisa was described, in Chapter 1, as sullen and withdrawn. She did not put forth effort in her work. Her teacher stated that she might not be able to attend to her work because she might be "too upset to focus on it." It is possible that Lisa has an attention-deficit hyperactivity disorder, predominantly inattentive type, with symptoms of inattention and lack of persistence on tasks. A more complete evaluation would need to be conducted to see whether she meets other criteria for this diagnosis.

With regard to Evan, who often called out in class, expressed annoyance with having to complete classwork, and often left his seat to sharpen his pencil or left the room to go to the bathroom, he displays some symptoms that are consistent with an attention-deficit hyperactivity disorder, predominantly hyperactive-impulsive type. Once again, the symptoms exhibited by both of these children can raise questions about the possibility that they are suffering from symptoms related to numerous diagnoses. It is important to wait for a complete assessment before assuming that ADHD exists.

Associated Symptoms

ADHD symptoms can often overlap with symptoms found in other disorders, and ADHD may coexist with other diagnoses (Monastra, Lubar, & Linden, 2001). According to Monastra and colleagues (2001), it is not unusual for individuals diagnosed with ADHD to also suffer from a conduct disorder or affective disorder. ADHD is also reported to have been diagnosed in "at least 50% of clinic-referred individuals with Tourette's Disorder" (APA, 2000, p. 88).

In a sample of South African children, Slone and colleagues (1996) stated that ADHD was associated with "disciplinary problems, social impairment, aggression, and impulsiveness" (p. 200). The American Psychiatric Association (2000) also notes that behavioral and emotional characteristics (e.g., "low frustration tolerance," "mood lability," "poor self-esteem"; pp. 87–88) may be evident in some ADHD children. As noted earlier, ADHD may occur in isolation or coexist with other diagnoses; in addition, the symptoms of ADHD may actually be caused by another disorder (e.g., inattention may be part of depression).

ANDY: DIAGNOSED WITH BOTH ADHD AND DEPRESSION

Ten-year-old Andy had been referred to the school-based team of specialists by his teacher, Mr. Gold. Mr. Gold informed the team that Andy was easily irritated by his peers, cried when frustrated or when he did not immediately understand his work, and often appeared to be agitated as he paced around the classroom. Mr. Gold commented that he would not have referred Andy to the team since he still had some strategies he wanted to try to implement within the room, except for the fact that Andy had recently started making alarming statements. Mr. Gold explained that Andy has been referring to himself as an "idiot" for most of the year when his work was incorrect, and he had informed his teacher that he lacks friends because "I'm not normal." This past week, his comments increased in intensity. Andy stated that "everybody would be happier if I was dead." Mr. Gold was concerned that Andy might try to harm himself.

The school-based team agreed that such statements should not be left uninvestigated by a trained mental health professional. In fact, the school psychologist noted that such statements should be reported the same day they are verbalized so that the potential for follow-through on self-destructive plans can be ameliorated. The specialists initially suspected that Andy was suffering from low self-esteem and depression. After his mother and father met with the school psychologist and described Andy's history of impulsivity, restlessness, and lack of patience, the possibility of either ADHD symptoms leading to secondary depression or the presence of both ADHD and depression was considered. Andy's mother had a history of clinical depression and had been taking antidepressant medication for several years. Although she denied that Andy would have knowledge of this, she did acknowledge that some of his self-perceptions (e.g., exaggerating his negative characteristics and minimizing his strengths) were similar to her own ways of looking at herself.

Andy received an evaluation by the school psychologist and then by a child psychiatrist. He was diagnosed with ADHD as well as with a major depressive disorder. The psychiatrist was concerned about the depressive symptoms but did not feel that hospitalization was immediately required. Andy received intensive outpatient psychotherapy, school-based counseling, modifications of his class assignments (so that he could meet with greater success), and medication. This combination of interventions proved to be effective.

Andy's, Claude's, and Martin's symptoms illustrate some of the ways in which ADHD can be manifested. Marshall (1989) comments that there are likely to be many different underlying causes of ADHD, especially given the multitude of ways in which the disorder can be manifested. In my professional experience, it is also important to consider how the child's personality, relationships, and environment influence the way the disorder is displayed.

ADHD and Allergies—Is There a Connection? There is the possibility that factors such as allergies may create or exaggerate symptoms consistent with ADHD. The relationship between allergies and ADHD has been studied in the literature. Although some professionals firmly assert that there is a relationship between ADHD symptoms and allergic disorders, McGee, Stanton, and Sears (1993) found "little support" for the connection between allergies and ADHD in their study of children (p. 85).

Marshall (1989) proposed:

> It is possible that very severe allergic reactions in some individuals may precipitate clinically significant changes in arousal and attentional behaviors. . . . It is more likely that, in most individuals, these reactions interact with other variables to produce clinically significant behaviors. For instance, the neurochemical processes resulting from allergic reactions . . . may interact with a preexisting poor modulation of arousal resulting from weak frontal lobe function with a genetic basis, or even more likely, these neurochemical reactions may interact with those generated by psychological stress. (p. 443)

Physiological Findings Associated with ADHD

Although there is no proof-positive laboratory test for diagnosing ADHD (Monastra et al., 2001), research studies have explored physiological correlates of this disorder. According to the American Psychiatric Association (2000), "minor physical anomalies (e.g., hypertelorism, highly arched palate, low-set ears) may occur at a higher rate" in those with ADHD than in those who do not meet the diagnostic criteria for this disorder (p. 89). In my direct contact with ADHD individuals, however, this pattern has not been noted. The absence of such physical features, therefore, should not deter a teacher from speaking with mental health professionals about concerns about a student's symptoms of inattention, hyperactivity, and/or impulsivity.

Monastra and colleagues (2001) report that research studies have used "a variety of neuroimaging techniques" that have "observed metabolic . . . circulatory . . . and neuroanatomical . . . differences between individuals diagnosed with ADHD and same-age peers without neurological impairment" (p. 137). These authors utilized electroencephalographic (QEEG) examinations on the children in their research project. These investigators indicated "that although evidence of cortical slowing of the vertex and over frontal cortical sites is commonly noted during QEEG examination of patients with ADHD, it is not found in all patients with ADHD" (p. 143).

Doyle, Biederman, Seidman, Weber, and Faraone (2000) comment that neuropsychological test results suggest that ADHD children may have deficits in frontal lobe functioning. Similarly, Seidman, Biederman, Faraone, Weber, and Ouellette (1997) found support for a possible dysfunction of the frontal area of the brain in ADHD youngsters. However, they note that there is no certain causal relationship between frontal area dysfunction and ADHD.

Other researchers have also found physiological factors that may be related to ADHD. Barry, Lyman, and Klinger (2002) reviewed some of the literature on this topic and note that children with ADHD appear to have somewhat different MRI (magnetic resonance imaging) findings than a group of children without this diagnosis. These authors state that MRI results have revealed that children with ADHD have symmetrical frontal lobes with a decrease in the blood flow in these lobes, while other youngsters show differences in the sizes of their frontal lobes, with the right side being slightly larger than the left, and no such decrease in blood flow.

According to Aman and colleagues (1998), the prefrontal areas of the frontal lobes appear to play an important role in "planning and implementing goal-oriented strategies, controlling impulses, inhibiting prepotent responses, shifting and maintaining strategy sets, and organizing and implementing search strategies" (p. 956). Many of these functions (known as *executive functions*) have been reported to be challenges for ADHD students.

Barry and colleagues (2002), however, studied ADHD children and found that they "did not exhibit significant impairments in" areas of executive function (p. 277). Therefore, it is recommended that teachers understand this information but wait for further evidence to clarify the relationship between brain attributes and ADHD symptoms. Even when physiological patterns are noted to differentiate ADHD from control groups of children, such differences may not differentiate all ADHD children from those without the disorder.

Further Studies About the Nature of ADHD

In addition to studies on the physiology of ADHD, there have been other theories about this disorder. Zentall (1993), for instance, notes:

> Attention "deficit" is more accurately described as attentional "bias" . . . [because] an attention deficit connotes a lack of attention, where as attentional bias more correctly connotes adequate attention, memory, and comprehension, but associated with specific tasks, time periods, and conditions. (p. 143)

Zentall also reports that "students with ADHD selectively attend to novelty, such as color, changes in size, and movement" (p. 143). Perhaps this explains why so many ADHD students have informed me that they have highly developed attention to any hallway noises yet struggle to listen to long lessons, and they like moving and interacting with material while completing classwork (e.g., hands-on learning, role playing).

ADHD has received significant research attention during the past 10 years. Barkley (1997), for instance, reports:

> Substantial evidence points to an impairment in three processes involving behavioral inhibition in ADHD: inhibition of prepotent responses, stopping of ongoing responses given feedback on errors, and interference control. (p. 87)

Barkley defines a "prepotent response . . . as that response for which immediate reinforcement (positive or negative) is available or has been previously associated with that response" (pp. 68–69) and interference control as the sustaining of the period of response delay "and the self-directed responses that occur within it from disruption by competing events and responses" (p. 68). He notes that the following components appear to be problematic areas in ADHD: "behavioral inhibition, working memory, poor self-regulation of motivation, and motor control and sequencing" (p. 87).

Nigg (2001) states that there is disagreement in the literature and among researchers as to whether there is an inhibitory difficulty in those suffering from ADHD. An inhibitory challenge may make it more difficult for the ADHD student to inhibit impulsive desires or actions. Nigg notes that the disagreement may stem from the lack of a clearly defined construct for inhibition. This author also states that some investigators propose alternative explanations for understanding ADHD, such as "state moderators of performance . . . [that can include] arousal, activation, or effort . . . regulation . . . alertness, or vigilance systems . . . and response style or time estimation ability" (p. 571). Nigg concludes by reporting that "the evidence in the executive domain suggests that the ADHD deficit has more to do with inhibition than with strength of prepotent impulse" (p. 592). Therefore, it is proposed that the ADHD student may not experience stronger needs, for instance, than peers, but may have more difficulty surpressing them.

Zentall (1993) reviewed the literature to assess the possible effects of ADHD on a student's school functioning. Zentall notes that ADHD children "are more likely than children without disabilities to receive lower grades in academic subjects" (p. 143). Since this disorder can directly impact a child in the classroom, the teacher may notice symptoms and question whether an assessment is indicated.

As previously stated, ADHD can involve many different behavioral manifestations, including inattention, impulsivity, and hyperactivity. Each of these symptom categories can create difficulty for a child when he or she is in a classroom setting with many other students, needs to wait to take a turn at certain activities, may be asked to listen to a lesson for a period of time that exceeds the length of his or her attention span, may call out in class, or may have trouble staying still and sitting behind a desk.

Throughout this book, the benefits of having a multidisciplinary evaluation for children have been highlighted. Monastra and colleagues (2001) also report that an ADHD evaluation might include a multidimensional assessment, including "a detailed review of medical, developmental, social, family, and academic histories and the use of behavioral ratings provided by multiple observers" (p. 136). Medical history is important to rule out medical symptoms that may mimic ADHD symptoms, the developmental history is important because some symptoms are generally noted to be evident prior to the age of 7, and family history is important because research suggests that ADHD is "more common in the first-degree biological relatives" of those already diagnosed (APA, 2000, p. 90).

Behavior Rating Scales in an ADHD Assessment

The use of behavioral rating scales, which are often normed, can be completed by adults in various settings of the child's life. Since the American Psychiatric Association (2000) states that the ADHD symptoms must negatively impact functioning in at least two settings, it is important to determine whether difficulties occur only in school, only at home, in both settings, or in other environments. When an evaluator reviews rating scales, the possibility of rater bias should be considered if all ratings are consistent with the exception of one rater's scores, which are dramatically different. For instance, one rater may believe that it is kinder to minimize symptoms than to report the numerous areas of dysfunction that are evident. Another rater may have an extremely high tolerance for the impulsive child and not believe that the child's symptoms are abnormal.

I have had the experience, on a number of occasions, of a child in fourth, fifth, or sixth grade being referred for an ADHD evaluation. In the course of the assessment, behavioral questionnaires were given to each teacher, starting with the child's kindergarten teacher. Each of the educators reported that they had a clear memory of the particular student and felt comfortable completing the paperwork. This historical study has provided valuable information on the child's development, compared to the peer group that the inventory was normed on, and on whether the symptoms were becoming more apparent, less atypical, or remaining constant. At times, the gap appears to widen as the expectations for increased attention, organization, or patience rise.

The historical review may also show that in one grade the student was rated as having many symptoms of ADHD while no other teacher reported concerns. Or the converse could be true as well. In such cases, it is important to look at the way each classroom environment is structured and the tolerance levels of each teacher for hyperactive, impulsive, or inattentive behaviors. One teacher may see hyperactive symptoms, for instance, but not view them as problematic, but rather as a sign of exuberance.

Suggestions for Teachers: Helping ADHD Students

Once a child is diagnosed with ADHD, there are numerous strategies (and numerous books highlighting them) that the classroom teacher can utilize to assist the student.

STRATEGIES TO HELP ADHD STUDENTS

- If the student is inattentive, it may be helpful to call the child by name, to focus him or her, before asking a direct question.
- To address hyperactive restlessness, it is sometimes helpful to send the student on errands at points during the day when restlessness is most problematic. This may decrease the level of overactivity that can occur, while channeling the energy into adaptive movements.
- If a child is impulsive, this may be evident when he or she quickly completes tasks without checking them. Some students benefit from a small checklist that they can review before turning in the work. Other children, however, do not find the checklist to be helpful but find behavioral incentives and a behavior-modification program beneficial.

Each teacher may need to experiment with ways to help the identified child. Often, the teacher, parent, and school mental health professional can collaborate to develop a program that offers the best plan for that student. In addition, some ADHD students may benefit from social skills and organizational skill-building activities that help them to feel better about themselves.

If a student is on medication (there are numerous kinds of medications now used for this disorder), the medicating doctor may be more effective in modulating the dose if the teacher can provide concrete feedback on how it is working. This may include information on improvements, times during the day that the child is most focused and able to complete work, times that are most difficult for the student, and any negative observations—such as tics, increased irritability, and so on. In order to keep the parent informed, these observations should be shared with the parent and then, if the parent gives permission, shared with the medicating professional.

The Positive Characteristics of ADHD Children

Zentall (1993) comments on the positive characteristics of many ADHD children, stating that "we . . . need to recognize the potential energy, creativity, leadership, and spontaneity of students with ADHD when determining accommodations for them" (p. 150). Just as intervention plans are based on areas of difficulty, the most effective intervention strategies are those that emphasize a student's strengths, build self-esteem, and involve the student in the formulation of the plan to the extent that is realistic for that child.

OPPOSITIONAL DEFIANT DISORDER (ODD)

It is not uncommon for a teacher or a parent to seek an appointment with me to complain that a child is "acting defiantly" or is "stubborn." When these characteristics persist for an extended period of time, the youngster may benefit from an assessment to determine if an oppositional defiant disorder is present. The following example illustrates this point.

MARYANN: ARGUMENTATIVE

Ten-year-old Maryann, for example, was described by her teacher as "manipulative, argumentative, and uncooperative" because she frequently argued about the value of assignments given to her in class. She also rarely completed her work. When questioned, Maryann would report that she forgot about the work or that another student prevented her from completing it or she just felt that the assignment wasn't "worth my time." Maryann's father noted that Maryann also did not follow through on responsibilities at home, such as completing chores and finishing her homework. At home, Maryann was often argumentative, as she questioned and broke rules and commented that her siblings got more "respect" and more "freedom." Maryann's father described her as the child who always questions decisions, debates most rules, and is often irritable and spiteful. He informed a consulting psychologist that these behaviors had been evident for almost a year. After a thorough evaluation, it was determined that Maryann met the criteria for ODD.

Defining ODD

Maryann's personality and behavioral characteristics are not atypical for some children who are going through the "terrible twos" or adolescence. However, when they are evident in an age-inappropriate fashion and last for more than 6 months (APA, 2000), then there is the possibility that the student has an oppositional defiant disorder.

According to the American Psychiatric Association (2000) definition of this disorder, a student must display at least four of the following symptoms:

> often loses temper; often argues with adults; often actively defies or refuses to comply with adults' requests or rules; often deliberately annoys people; often blames others for his or her mistakes or misbehaviors; is often touchy or easily annoyed by others; is often angry and resentful; is often spiteful or vindictive. (p. 102)

Shabad (2000) offers an explanation for why a person might appear to be spiteful. The author states that spite is displayed when a person feels the shame of being powerless and then concludes that he or she will not be able to control a given situation. The person uses spite rather than an outwardly directed assertiveness "to recapture one's individual dignity through an opposition to power on which one depends and by which one feels entrapped" (p. 690). Spite may be evident in the home but not in school, although the reverse can also occur, and sometimes the symptoms are present in multiple settings.

The Research

According to the American Psychiatric Association (2000), the prevalence rate of this disorder, which is also sometimes referred to as "OD" or as "ODD," is reported to be 2 to 16 percent. There appears to be an increased prevalence in those preschool males who have "high reactivity" and "difficulty being soothed" or "high motor activity. During the school years, there may be low self-esteem, . . . mood lability, low frustration tolerance, swearing, and the precocious use of alcohol, tobacco, or illicit drugs" (APA, 2000, p. 100).

In a study by Ford and colleagues (1999), an association was found between oppositional defiant disorder and a history of having been victimized, although the authors could not determine whether "ODD and trauma are causally linked and in what direction(s)" (p. 789). Lindahl (1998) also looked at correlates of this disorder and found that "levels of family and marital conflict, marital dissatisfaction, and marital hostility tended to be high—much higher" in the oppositional defiant disordered group "than in the control group" (p. 433) and that the families of these children "were found to be the most lax and inconsistent and the least cohesive" (p. 433) of the groups assessed.

Suggestions for Teachers: Helping Students with ODD

Based on these findings, it would seem to follow that a student would likely benefit from a classroom environment that has clear, consistent rules and a nurturing atmosphere that values individuality and shared decision making. In addition, after reviewing the information described earlier by Shabad (2000), teachers might consider offering ODD students specific ways to gain feelings of empowerment without overwhelming them with requirements of independence; this may help decrease tensions and symptoms for some individuals.

Carlos became more cooperative after his teacher allowed him to decide whether he would complete a multiple-choice test along with his classmates or whether he would communicate his understanding of the information through an essay. Carlos was also given an opportunity to help younger students in resolving conflicts. While there was an adult there to supervise his input, Carlos saw this experience as one that allowed him to be respected by the younger students and to feel competent to resolve conflicts in an adaptive manner.

There are often times when a teacher can create options for youngsters who tend to become defiant when given specific directives. Many students, such as Carlos, benefit from experiencing the power of negotiating in some areas and then become more cooperative when an adult's decision is nonnegotiable. When symptoms are not ameliorated by classroom intervention strategies, the teacher might consult with the child's parent and with the school-based mental health staff to determine whether more intensive assessment or treatment is indicated.

LISA AND EVAN: DO THEY HAVE ODD?

Let us return to our case examples of Lisa and Evan to see if there is evidence that they may each be suffering from ODD. Lisa appeared to be sullen and avoided completing tasks that were required by her teacher. Perhaps her lack of focus on finishing her work is a reflection of her overall refusal to comply with requirements set forth by authority figures. Evan was more directly argumentative and challenged the benefit of doing the work. However, as noted numerous times in earlier sections of this book, symptoms that overlap with a particular disorder can exist for other reasons. Evan and Lisa have behavioral characteristics that raise some question about the presence of ODD, but a more thorough assessment would be indicated before any conclusions could be reached.

ODD May Have Features Similar to Other Disorders

In regard to symptoms of an oppositional defiant disorder, a child with post-traumatic stress disorder (PTSD) can exhibit many of these characteristics as a reaction to trauma, a depressed child can be irritable as a result of the depression, a child with language deficits may have difficulty following through on verbal requests because of struggles to process and remember the information rather than out of a desire to rebel, and a child with ADHD may become frustrated and angry when asked to complete work that requires sustained attention and, thus, ignore the work.

Waldman and Lilienfeld (1991) reviewed some of the literature on oppositional defiant disorder and stated that there is a moderate correlation between this disorder and ADHD and a somewhat higher correlation between this disorder and conduct disorders. Loeber, Lahey, and Thomas (1991), however, state that

> most symptoms of CD and ODD are distinct . . . [although] mild physical aggression and lying seem to be related to both CD and ODD. . . . It is also probably the case that ODD preceded the onset of CD . . . [especially in light of the fact that the] mean age of onset for ODD symptoms is earlier than that for CD symptoms. (p. 387)

The next section highlights some of the symptoms and characteristics of a conduct disorder.

CONDUCT DISORDER (CD)

Defining CD

A "conduct disorder (CD) is a pattern of maladaptive behavior of children that is characterized by a variety of antisocial behaviors, including physical aggression, deception, and violations of property rights of others" (Lahey et al., 1995, p. 83).

The term delinquency has been associated with conduct-disordered children and adolescents. Brier (1995) defines delinquency as "a legal term to indicate that the youngster has engaged in illegal activities and as a clinical term to indicate that the youngster is displaying a pattern of conduct disordered behavior" (p. 272).

A student diagnosed with this disorder seriously violates societal rules. On the surface, then, this disorder would be easily diagnosed based on observable behaviors, such as cruelty to other living creatures, deliberately setting fires, and stealing. However, the case descriptions of John and Richard in Chapter 3 illustrate the challenge of determining whether the diagnosis is valid for an individual child or children.

JOHN AND RICHARD: DISORDERED OR JUST TRYING TO SURVIVE?

John and Richard were living on the street with their younger siblings and their mother. Their mother had difficulty caring for her children, and she abused drugs daily. John and Richard burglarized grocery stores at night and stole food, and they robbed people for money, but only when they needed food to feed their family or when they needed to purchase essential items for family members. They never attended school because they had no permanent residence, and they felt that they needed to be around their younger siblings to care for and protect them.

John and Richard reportedly did not like engaging in illegal actions and knew that society did not condone their behaviors. However, they felt that there were no alternatives. Since these actions were believed to be necessary for the survival of the family, based on John's and Richard's assessment of their situation, one can argue that they are not conduct-disordered youngsters but, rather, desperate individuals trying to be responsible *despite* their obvious violations against society. The American Psychiatric Association (2000) notes that extenuating circumstances may lead to actions that mimic but do not lead to the diagnosis of a conduct disorder.

The Research

There are many children who qualify for, and are diagnosed with, a conduct disorder. The incidence rate for this disorder has been reported to range "from less than 1% to more than 10%" and "prevalence rates are higher among males than females" (APA, 2000, p. 97). Some research findings suggest that youth with a conduct disorder may view the world as more hostile and aggressive than do other children. For instance, Dodge, Price, Bachorowski, and Newman (1990) studied adolescent boys in a maximum security prison. They found a correlation between their "severity of undersocialized aggressive conduct disorder . . . [and their inclination] to attribute hostile intent to peer antagonists" (p. 390). The authors emphasize, however, that their results point to a correlation between the disorder and the attribution style but do not prove causation (e.g., perceptions of hostile intent by others leading to the disorder, or vice versa). The relationship between aggressive youngsters and their tendency to have a preconceived perception of hostility in others is also noted by Yoon, Hughes, Cavell, and Thompson (2000). In addition, Yoon and colleagues comment that these children tend to find aggressive methods of problem resolution.

Conduct Disorders, Mood, and Interpersonal Skills. Many studies have explored correlates of conduct disorders. Lahey and colleagues (1995) found that persistence of conduct disorder symptoms seem to be positively correlated with a "below-average verbal intelligence" (p. 91). In another study, Sanders, Dadds, Johnston, and Cash (1992) found that during a discussion that focused on problem solving, conduct-disordered youngsters did not have the same level of adaptive or effective use of language and were more likely to use nonadaptive verbalizations when they were compared to children not diagnosed with a conduct disorder. Sanders and colleagues (1992) also found that youngsters with a conduct disorder showed "elevated levels of" anger and revealed signs "of depressive affect during family discussions" (p. 502). These results reconfirm my assertion that symptoms of disorders can overlap and even a child with a particular behavioral presentation (e.g., aggression or defiance) may have feelings (e.g., depression) that the observer may find surprising and unanticipated. Overall, Sanders and colleagues (1992) suggest that children diagnosed with a conduct disorder also display a deficiency in "interpersonal problem solving skills" (p. 502).

The association found between children with conduct disorders and the presence of difficulties with verbal problem resolution skills in the study conducted by Sanders and colleagues (1992) raises questions about whether communication struggles might lead some children to feel frustrated when they do not experience the power of words. Certainly not all children with language difficulties are going to develop antisocial behaviors, even if they do experience frustration because of their language deficits. In my professional experience, there have been situations where a child displayed both difficulties, but the large majority of language-impaired youngsters do not show signs of a conduct disorder.

JIMMY: POSSIBLE IMPACT OF VERBAL SKILL DEFICITS

However, in the case of 8-year-old Jimmy, his behavioral difficulties escalated over time and appeared to be at least partially related to his verbal skill deficits. Jimmy often stole things from his peers, was once caught rummaging through his teacher's pocketbook, frequently initiated fights on the playground, periodically tore up essays or homework completed by other students, and even threatened to hurt another child (a straight-A student) one day if the other child didn't do his homework for him. When questioned by the school principal, and later by his mother, about the threat to harm his classmate, Jimmy would only say, "I didn't do anything really bad."

Jimmy's mother met with the principal, with the school psychologist, and with a police officer who was following up on a parent's complaint that Jimmy had threatened her son. Two steps were immediately taken. The school psychologist, along with a consulting psychiatrist who came to the school when needed, met with Jimmy to assess whether he was dangerous to himself or to others and whether he needed immediate psychiatric hospitalization. Later, the police officer met with Jimmy, in the presence of his mother, to discuss the seriousness of his threat and antisocial behaviors.

In the follow-up meeting, which occurred later that same day, it was decided that Jimmy was not in need of hospitalization but should immediately begin psychotherapy with a qualified mental health professional to explore his anger, his apparent lack of empathy for others, and his impulse control issues. The school principal said that Jimmy would be suspended for a three-day period due to his threatening statement and repeated incidents of physical aggression. The police officer reported that further legal involvement might follow if the parents of the other child pressed charges.

Jimmy's mother was uncomfortable having Jimmy receive school-based counseling or private psychotherapy because she believed that she and her husband should be able to help their own son. After further discussion, she agreed to both of these interventions because of the seriousness of her son's recent actions. However, she also wanted to be actively involved in helping Jimmy.

During Jimmy's suspension, his mother was able to schedule a screening for him at a local clinic to determine what kind of therapy would be appropriate. The psychiatrist who screened Jimmy felt that he needed to enter treatment as soon as possible. She arranged for Jimmy to return that evening to meet with a psychologist to begin therapy. Jimmy reluctantly agreed. During the next few therapy sessions, the therapist realized that Jimmy had difficulty using words to communicate many experiences and feelings. When she gently asked Jimmy if he ever felt like it was hard to use words to let others know what he was thinking, Jimmy admitted that this was an area of difficulty for him.

His therapist then went one step further to test a theory she had developed. She asked Jimmy to try to talk with her about what happens in school during the periods immediately before, during, and after the times that he engages in the maladaptive actions. Jimmy initially responded with his typical statement of, "I don't know. I don't care. I just do stuff." However, with further encouragement to talk about the school situation, Jimmy eventually began crying and stated that "I'm just a bad kid; I'm totally messed up." He then gave his therapist insight into the feelings and thoughts that he experienced immediately prior to many of his incidents of physical aggression and stealing.

Apparently Jimmy became angry and aggressive when he felt that his classmates or his teacher seemed to ignore something he was trying to communicate or when he experienced the frustration of being unable to put his needs and wants into words. Then, when he took something from the individual who misunderstood him, or became physically aggressive toward the person, Jimmy felt satisfied that he had made the other person feel bad as well. Jimmy and his therapist asked Jimmy's mother to join the session, and they all discussed this information. With her son's permission, his mother shared the content of Jimmy's revelation with the school principal and counselor.

The school staff, along with Jimmy's mother (and at the suggestion of the therapist), decided to have Jimmy assessed for a possible language disability. Jimmy eagerly participated, as he hoped that someone would finally help him, now that he was emotionally available for the intervention. Jimmy was found to have significant areas of language deficit. He then began to receive special education services in school, his mother enrolled him in a school-based social skills group, and he continued in therapy at the clinic to address his depressive symptoms, anger management struggles, and difficulty empathizing with others. Almost immediately, his antisocial actions decreased and Jimmy admitted to feeling happier about himself. Jimmy was also relieved to hear that no legal charges were being pressed against him. He promised himself that he would never have to face another police officer because of his behavioral transgressions.

Conduct Disorder and Depression. Jimmy's history revealed antisocial behavior, language deficits, and depressive symptoms (e.g., low self-esteem). Returning to Sanders and colleagues' (1992) comments, they noted that children with a conduct disorder in their study also displayed "elevated levels of depressive affect during family discussions" (p. 502). The link among depressive symptoms, suicidal thoughts, and bullying behaviors has been reported in other research articles as well. Kaltiala-Heino and colleagues (1999) studied adolescents and found that "there was an increased prevalence of depression and severe suicidal ideation among . . . those who were bullies" (p. 348).

Hillbrand (2001) reviewed the literature and concluded that it is not uncommon for individuals who have externalized aggression also to display internalized aggression. An example of externalized aggression is when a youngster acts aggressively, through words or actions, against others. According to Hillbrand, these same children frequently turn their hostility against themselves. The internalization of aggression can result in depression, self-berating actions, and low self-esteem. Jimmy displayed anger both toward himself and toward others. Incidents of suicide-homicide that have been reported in the press are an extreme example of how an individual can be aggressive both to self and to others. Hillbrand, therefore, recommends that "risk assessment for suicide and homicide should go hand in hand" (p. 632).

Conduct Disorder and Impulsivity. White and colleagues (1994) report that there is a higher frequency of delinquency among children with impulsive behaviors. These authors speculate that this relationship may exist because of the children's inability "to control or monitor their behavior" (p. 202). These impulsive, delinquent youngsters may engage in such actions as stealing and spontaneous fighting if they perceive that an immediate reward will result from their actions and only negligible "negative consequences" (White et al., 1994, p. 202).

ARTHUR: DIAGNOSED WITH A CONDUCT DISORDER AND ADHD

White and colleagues' description accurately described the underlying difficulties that 11-year-old Arthur displayed. Arthur was frequently in trouble for defacing school property with his graffiti, destroying the projects of his peers, breaking windows for no apparent reason, intimidating other students, and fighting at recess. His mother spoke with his teacher about these school-based concerns and then admitted that she had her own difficulties with Arthur. She explained that he runs away from home whenever there are limits set on him, he once threw a stray cat across the lawn because it trespassed into their backyard, and he breaks objects around the house when angry.

Whenever Arthur was questioned about his behaviors, he feigned innocence and reported, "I thought it was OK" or "It's no big deal anyway." When consequences ensued, Arthur became upset, saying, "I forgot I'd get in trouble, OK?" He would then try to avoid the penalty by saying, "I'm sorry. Can we just forget it now?"

Arthur had been in therapy for over a month, without improvement in his behavior. His therapist wondered whether Arthur had difficulty containing his impulses because of an attention-deficit hyperactivity disorder (ADHD). A psychiatrist confirmed her suspicions and diagnosed Arthur with a conduct disorder along with ADHD. Based on the recommendations of the mental heath professionals, Arthur's mother agreed to let her son begin a trial period on medication to see if it would help him.

Once he was on medication, the intensity of Arthur's negative actions decreased significantly. However, he still acted impulsively when there was no immediate consequence for his behavior. The long-term consequences (e.g., continued episodes of stealing and defacing school property would lead to possible transfer to a smaller, more structured classroom setting away from his two friends) did not appear to affect his behavior. Arthur's teacher and psychologist collaborated to develop a behavior-modification chart for him, after consulting with Arthur's parents.

The behavior-modification system segmented his day into 30-minute periods. At the end of each period, Arthur received an index card for prosocial actions, no card for neutral actions, and a card with "–1" written on it for antisocial actions. At the end of the day, Arthur counted up his index cards, subtracted the number of minus cards, and then received either a small reinforcer or a negative consequence (if left with a negative number). At the end of the week, he could have his favorite dinner if he had earned a certain number of points on his cards throughout the week.

This combination of immediate consequences and long-term reinforcers, plus the continued use of medication and participation in therapy, was effective in helping Arthur to curtail his impulsive actions. Later, Arthur admitted that he was surprised at "how easy" it was "to be good." Although this strategy may not be effective with all children, and some conduct-disordered students may rebel against the attempt to monitor their actions, many students have benefited from behavioral intervention plans.

As noted earlier, impulsivity, verbal problem-solving deficits, below-average IQ in the verbal area, and perceptions about the hostile intent of others have all been correlated with conduct disorders. In my therapeutic work with conduct-disordered children and adolescents, they have shared their subjective views regarding why they engage in antisocial activities. These comments include: "I get respect. Nobody messes with me because they're afraid of me!" "I took it because I didn't have it. I wanted it." "That kid deserves to be hurt." "It feels good to hit people." "I feel better than everyone because I can do what I want." "I can't help it." "I need help." "I have no control." "I just can't seem to help it." "It's because my parents are so mean." "It's because my parents work too much." Each child may have a unique spin on why the conduct-disordered behaviors are exhibited. For each child, an intervention plan that is specifically tailored to his or her personality, situation, and goals may need to be developed.

It is important to keep in mind that many of the children who report that their antisocial actions are acceptable to them may actually feel happier if able to attain "status" and "control" in a more prosocial manner. They resort to the less adaptive actions because of emotional, social, cognitive, environmental, or other factors that come together to create their unique difficulties. Depending on which factor(s) lead to these difficulties, the reasons behind the behavior can be quite different for different children, even if they have displayed identical antisocial actions.

Up until this point, the cited literature has described associated features of conduct disorders rather than causes of the antisocial behaviors. When studying the potential causes of a child becoming persistently "violent," Dodge and colleagues (1997) conclude that there is no clear evidence that shows that one's life experience is the sole cause of aggressive patterns of behavior. These authors comment that though one's past experiences may contribute to the development of inappropriate patterns of aggression, it is also possible that one's physiological tendency toward having an aggressive nature may influence the way one interacts with the world, thus affecting one's life experiences.

Bullying

Before concluding this discussion about conduct disorders, it is important to spend some time focusing on bullying behaviors (in Chapter 4, the effects of bullying on victims was explored). According to Olweus (1994), bullying is one aspect of a more general pattern of antisocial behaviors. However, there is not always one distinct *bully* and another distinct *victim*. Some individuals are both bullies and victims.

Olweus (1994) defines bullying with

> three criteria: (a) It is aggressive behavior or intentional "harm doing" (b) which is carried out "repeatedly and over time" (c) in an interpersonal relationship characterized by an imbalance of power.... A distinctive characteristic of the typical bullies is their aggression toward peers . . . they are often characterized by impulsivity and a strong need to dominate others . . . [and these children are more likely to be aggressive if they are] active . . . [and have a] "hot-headed" temperament. (pp. 1173, 1180, 1182)

Olweus (1994) also comments that these individuals may come from families where there is a "lack of warmth and involvement . . . permissiveness towards aggressive behaviors . . . [or where there is] physical punishment and violent emotional outbursts" (p. 1182).

Types of Bullies. Twemlow, Sacco, and Williams (1996) differentiate bullies into three categories:

1. *The sadistic bully*, who does not tend to empathize with the victims, is not generally concerned about the possible consequences of actions, can enjoy causing distress in others, and demonstrates impulsivity
2. *The depressed bully*, who suffers from a negative self-image, "whines, tattles, and has aggressive outbursts"
3. *The agitated bully*, who suffers from anxiety and may have symptoms that are consistent with an attention deficit disorder, with or without hyperactivity (p. 304).

Twemlow and colleagues (1996) added that the particular bully type and the particular victim type interact with results that may vary depending upon this combination.

Gangs. While a single individual may engage in antisocial activities, or a small group of students may violate school rules, a few words should be said here in regard to gangs. Students who are gang members may have a strong desire to conform and follow rules, but they may be loyal to the gang's rules and not to the rules set forth by the classroom teacher or by the community at large.

Lopez and Emmer (2002) studied teenage male subjects who were residing in a treatment facility or a halfway house placement. The authors concluded that gang members' behaviors often adhere to clearly established rules set up by the gang and that violence is deemed to be acceptable by the group as a way to defend others, solve problems, and show loyalty to the gang.

Although a teacher may not know that a particular child is a gang member, his or her antisocial activities may be the identifying marker that the student does not follow the rules of either the school or the local community. Conduct disorders, delinquency, and gang-related violence all are characterized by violations of societal rules. Therefore, if our case illustrations of Lisa and Evan are revisited, it would soon be apparent that Lisa does not steal, harm others, or engage in some of the other behaviors noted earlier in this section. While Evan may violate his teacher's class rule for everyone to respect each other and to try to master academic challenges, he does this in a way that is more descriptive of other difficulties (e.g., agitated depression, ADHD, oppositional defiant disorder, or an attempt to mask an underlying learning disability) than of the serious violations typically involved in conduct disorders.

Suggestions for Teachers: Helping Students with a Conduct Disorder

What can be done if a teacher has a student with a conduct disorder in the classroom? First of all, while teachers accept the responsibility of educating children, they also have a right to feel safe. If a student has threatened a teacher or another pupil, whether this threat was direct ("I'll make you pay!") or subtle and indirect ("You look tired; I hope that you don't trip and fall leaving school today"), the teacher should be aware of the school-based and legally based steps to take so that no one is harmed. *Physical safety must be of paramount importance.*

Interventions to Reduce Violence

There have been numerous research projects to address school violence. For instance, Mulvey and Cauffman (2001) comment that the best way to prevent violence in school is to develop a "positive and supportive" environment where the students feel comfortable to discuss their problems and where they can participate in "ongoing activities" (p. 800). These authors also note that if the school promotes an atmosphere in which the "students feel connected and trusted," it will permit students who are aware of possible upcoming trouble to inform the people "who can act to prevent it" (p. 800).

To address the research findings that conduct-disordered youth may be more likely to attribute hostile intent to others, Yoon and colleagues (2000) suggest using "social cognitive intervention" to address these perceptions along with the fact that there is the likelihood of negative repercussions in the future for aggressive actions (p. 566).

Conduct-disordered youth may be involved in numerous "systems," such as the criminal justice system, school system, foster care system, family system, and mental health system. When appropriate, communication among these systems can lead to a comprehensive, minimally fragmented response to the behavioral difficulties and emotional needs of children with this disorder.

CONCLUSION

To conclude, this chapter reviewed some of the externalized disorders, including attention-deficit hyperactivity disorder, oppositional defiant disorder, and conduct disorder. Characteristics of each disorder, along with relevant research to aid in more thoroughly understanding the nature of the symptoms, were presented. Although symptoms may be evident in the classroom, teachers are advised to seek out the team of specialists in the school building and communicate with the child's parents to determine whether the symptoms are truly due to these disorders or are primarily caused by other factors (as was the case for John and Richard). In the case illustrations of Jimmy and Arthur, the potential for dual diagnoses is highlighted.

REFERENCES

Aman, C. J., Roberts, R. J., & Pennington, B. F. (1998). A neuropsychological examination of the underlying deficit in attention deficit hyperactivity disorder: Frontal lobe versus right parietal lobe theories. *Developmental Psychology*, 34(5), 956–969.

American Psychiatric Association (APA). (2000). *Diagnostic and statistical manual of mental disorders: Fourth edition, DSM-IV-TR, text revision*. Washington, DC: Author.

Barkley, R. A. (1997). Behavioral inhibition, sustained attention, and executive functions: Constructing a unifying theory of ADHD. *Psychological Bulletin*, 121(1), 65–94.

Barkley, R. A. (2000). *Taking charge of ADHD*. New York: Guilford.

Barry, T. D., Lyman, R. D., & Klinger, L. G. (2002). Academic underachievement and attention-deficit/hyperactivity disorder: The negative impact of symptom severity on school performance. *Journal of School Psychology*, 40(3), 259–283.

Brier, N. (1995). Predicting antisocial behavior in youngsters displaying poor academic achievement: A review of risk factors. *Developmental and Behavioral Pediatrics*, 16(4), 271–276.

Dodge, K. A., Lochman, J. E., Harnish, J. D., Bates, J. E., & Pettit, G. S. (1997). Reactive and proactive aggression in school children and psychiatrically impaired chronically assaultive youth. *Journal of Abnormal Psychology*, 106(1), 37–51.

Dodge, K. A., Price, J. M., Bachorowski, J., & Newman, J. P. (1990). Hostile attributional biases in severely aggressive adolescents. *Journal of Abnormal Psychology*, 99(4), 385–392.

Doyle, A. E., Biederman, J., Seidman, L. J., Weber, W., & Faraone, S. V. (2000). Diagnostic efficiency of neuropsychological test scores for discriminating boys with and without attention deficit-hyperactivity disorder. *Journal of Consulting and Clinical Psychology*, 68(3), 477–488.

Ford, J. D., Racusin, R., Daviss, W. B., Ellis, C. G., Thomas, J., Rogers, K., Reiser, J., Schiffman, J., & Sengupta, A. (1999). Trauma exposure among children with oppositional defiant disorder and attention-deficit hyperactivity disorder. *Journal of Consulting and Clinical Psychology*, 67(5), 786–789.

Hillbrand, M. (2001). Homicide-suicide and other forms of co-occurring aggression against self and against others. *Professional Psychology: Research and Practice*, 32(6), 626–635.

Kaltiala-Heino, R., Rimpela, M., Marttunen, M., Rimpela, A., & Rantanen, P. (1999). Bullying, depression, and suicidal ideation in Finnish adolescents: School survey. *British Medical Journal, 319*, 348–351.

Lahey, B., Loeber, R., Hart, E. L., Frick, P. J., Applegate, B., Zhang, Q., Green, S. M., & Russo, M. F. (1995). Four-year longitudinal study of conduct disorder in boys: Patterns and predictors of persistence. *Journal of Abnormal Psychology, 104*(1), 83–93.

Lindahl, K. M. (1998). Family process variables and children's disruptive behavior problems. *Journal of Family Psychology, 12*(3), 420–436.

Loeber, R., Lahey, B. B., & Thomas, C. (1991). Diagnostic conundrum of oppositional defiant disorder and conduct disorder. *Journal of Abnormal Psychology, 100*(3), 379–390.

Lopez, V. A., & Emmer, E. T. (2002). Influences of beliefs and values on male adolescents' decision to commit violent offenses. *Psychology of Men and Masculinity, 3*(1), 28–40.

Marshall, P. (1989). Attention deficit disorder and allergy: A neurochemical model of the relation between the illnesses. *Psychological Bulletin, 106*(3), 434–446.

McGee, R., Stanton, W. R., & Sears, M. R. (1993). Allergic disorders and attention deficit disorder in children. *Journal of Abnormal Child Psychology, 21*(1), 79–88.

Monastra, V. J., Lubar, J. F., & Linden, M. (2001). The development of a quantitative electroencephalographic scanning process for attention deficit-hyperactivity disorder: Reliability and validity studies. *Neuropsychology, 15*(1), 136–144.

Mulvey, E. P., & Cauffman, E. (2001). The inherent limits of predicting school violence. *American Psychologist, 56*(10), 797–802.

Nigg, J. T. (2001). Is ADHD a disinhibitory disorder? *Psychological Bulletin, 127*(5), 571–598.

Olweus, D. (1994). Annotation: Bullying at school: Basic facts and effects of a school based intervention program. *Journal of Child Psychology and Psychiatry, 35*(7), 1171–1190.

Sanders, M. R., Dadds, M. R., Johnston, B. M., & Cash, R. (1992). Childhood depression and conduct disorder: I. Behavioral, affective, and cognitive aspects of family problem-solving interactions. *Journal of Abnormal Psychology, 101*(3), 495–504.

Seidman, L. J., Biederman, J., Faraone, S. V., Weber, W., & Ouellette, C. (1997). Toward defining a neuropsychology of attention deficit-hyperactivity disorder: Performance of children and adolescents from a large clinically referred sample. *Journal of Consulting and Clinical Psychology, 65*(1), 150–160.

Shabad, P. (2000). Giving the devil his due: Spite and the struggle for individual dignity. *Psychoanalytic Psychology, 17*(4), 690–705.

Slone, M., Durrheim, K., & Kaminer, D. (1996). Attention deficit hyperactivity disorder: Clinical presentation and correlates in a South African sample. *Professional Psychology: Research and Practice, 27*(2), 198–201.

Twemlow, S. W., Sacco, F. C., & Williams, P. (1996). A clinical and interactionist perspective on the bully-victim-bystander relationship. *Bulletin of the Menninger Clinic, 60*(3), 296–313.

Waldman, I. D., & Lilienfeld, S. O. (1991). Diagnostic efficiency of symptoms for oppositional defiant disorder and attention-deficit hyperactivity disorder. *Journal of Consulting and Clinical Psychology, 59*(5), 732–738.

White, J. L., Moffitt, T. E., Caspi, A., Bartusch, D. J., Needles, D. J., & Stouthamer-Loeber, M. (1994). Measuring impulsivity and examining its relationship to delinquency. *Journal of Abnormal Psychology, 103*(2), 192–205.

Yoon, J. S., Hughes, J. N., Cavell, T. A., & Thompson, B. (2000). Social cognitive differences between aggressive-rejected and aggressive-nonrejected children. *Journal of School Psychology, 38*(6), 551–570.

Zentall, S. S. (1993). Research on the educational implications of attention deficit hyperactivity disorder. *Exceptional Children, 60*(2), 143–153.

CHAPTER 7

Additional Areas of Concern

Selective Mutism; Autism and Asperger's Disorder;
Tics and Tourette's Disorder; Psychosis; Eating Disorders;
The Atypical Child

In this chapter, numerous disorders, difficulties, and challenges that can impact children are explored. These include selective mutism, autism, Asperger's disorder (Asperger's syndrome), tics, Tourette's disorder (Tourette's syndrome), psychotic symptoms, eating disorders, and the atypical child who does not meet criteria for having a disorder.

SELECTIVE MUTISM

DANA: JUST SHY?

On the first day of school, 5-year-old Dana walked off her school bus with the other children and willingly entered her classroom. She was cooperative throughout the day as she followed classroom instructions and appeared to be attentive when her new teacher read the students a story from a book. Her teacher later asked the students to sit at their desks. Dana complied. However, her difficulties soon emerged. As the teacher pointed to each student, the student was expected to tell the others his or her name. When it came time for Dana to speak, Dana stared directly at her teacher but did not speak. Dana received encouragement to "Just tell your new friends who you are, OK?" Once again, Dana just looked at her teacher.

Dana's teacher initially felt that Dana was "shy" and decided to see whether she would start talking as she became more comfortable in the classroom. However, by the third week of school, Dana had not verbalized a single word. Now, her teacher was very concerned and decided to call Dana's mother to see whether Dana had a history of expressive language difficulties or other issues that might explain her non-verbal manner.

Dana's mother was not surprised to receive the phone call from her daughter's teacher. However, she had hoped that Dana might start the new school experience by communicating verbally to others, rather than continuing the silence that she had displayed throughout her time in preschool. Dana's teacher listened attentively during the phone conversation and learned that Dana had a history of not speaking in school and at parties. This nonverbal pattern had developed more than 18 months earlier, although her mother was unable to identify any precipitating factor that might have led to the behavior. Dana's mother described her daughter as verbally spontaneous at home and informed her teacher that Dana often spoke positively about school activities when she came home each day.

After learning that Dana had the ability to speak easily, but just not in certain situations, Dana's mother and teacher created a plan to assist her. They decided to have Dana's mother join the class on an upcoming field trip. In this context, Dana engaged in conversations with her mother, and other children learned that she had the ability to speak. Dana's mother also came to school frequently to help out in the building, with the goal of having Dana experience herself talking in school (even if it was just to her mother at first). In addition, Dana's mother arranged for Dana to have frequent playdates in her own home, where Dana was able to display her verbal skills directly to her peers. Over time, Dana began speaking at recess to those children with whom she had had playdates, and then she began speaking with those children and a few other students while she was in the classroom. However, since Dana continued to be nonverbal with her teacher, the school psychologist was consulted.

After conducting a comprehensive evaluation, the school psychologist diagnosed Dana as having selective mutism and suggested that a behavior-modification plan could be instituted whereby Dana would earn checks for each statement (beginning with whispers) to her teacher during the day. At the end of the day, her mother would give her varying forms of positive reinforcement, depending on the number of checks earned. To minimize chances of Dana experiencing pressure and negative reactions to the plan, no penalties were used for lack of speech. This positively oriented intervention plan was effective, as Dana gradually became more spontaneous when speaking individually to her teacher. While her teacher expressed some disappointment at the conclusion of the schoolyear that Dana had never volunteered to answer any questions in class and continued to be nonverbal when called on to respond to a discussion, this student had made significant progress.

ERIC: DEFIANT?

At times, a child's nonverbal behaviors can be viewed as a sign that the youngster is "stubborn," "controlling," or "defiant." Eric's first-grade teacher questioned whether his "refusal to speak" was due to his desire to gain attention and reflected defiance against the classroom expectation that children would participate verbally in discussions. Eric's behavior confused his teacher, since she had seen him speaking freely to his older brother as they walked off the bus and he engaged in all activities that did not require him to speak; nevertheless, he "refused" to speak to her or to classmates.

Eric's teacher met with the school counselor to try to understand Eric's behavior. Through the discussion, Eric's teacher learned about selective mutism and agreed to speak with his mother to learn whether Eric spoke in other environments (typical of children with selective mutism) or whether he never engaged in conversation except when he was around his older brother.

The school counselor followed up with the teacher the following week. The teacher informed the counselor that Eric's mother and father had met with her and told her that Eric had been diagnosed with selective mutism by a psychiatrist and took medication for this disorder. He was also in therapy to address his adjustment to the separation of his parents, which had occurred only a few weeks before the symptoms emerged.

The teacher, parents, and therapist spoke regularly and developed a system by which Eric initially agreed to answer "yes" or "no" to questions if he knew that no further verbalizations would be required. Gradually, he began to show further improvement but quickly regressed when his teacher called attention to his statements by praising him with phrases such as "Eric, thanks for talking. That was great!" His teacher learned how to assist Eric, and Eric learned how to begin to use words to communicate his knowledge of the school lessons and his personal needs. Eventually, Eric no longer displayed any signs of selective mutism, even after medication was discontinued.

Defining Selective Mutism

Selective mutism is reported to be a somewhat rare disorder (American Psychiatric Association [APA], 2000; Drewes & Akin-Little, 2002; Stone, Kratochwill, Sladezcek, & Serlin, 2002), occurring in less than 1 out of every 100, or 1 percent, of individuals (APA, 2000; Dow, Sonies, Schieb, Moss, & Leonard, 1995; Stone et al., 2002). The literature suggests that the disorder may be a bit more prevalent in girls than in boys (e.g., APA, 2000; Drewes & Akin-Little, 2002), although this may require further investigation (Dow et al., 1995).

Selective mutism is a disorder that is "characterized by the total lack of speech in at least one specific situation (usually the classroom), despite the ability to speak in other situations" (Dow et al., 1995, p. 836), and this lack of verbal communication significantly impacts functioning in that setting (APA, 2000).

The American Psychiatric Association (2000) states that the symptoms of selective mutism must be present for more than 1 month to meet diagnostic criteria ("not limited to the first month of school") (p. 127). Drewes and Akin–Little (2002) comment that the lack of verbalizations in a particular setting for "less than 1 month may simply be an adjustment reaction to a change in the environment, usually the beginning of school" (p. 42). This disorder typically develops before the age of 5 (APA, 2000), and symptoms may quickly dissipate. However, Drewes and Akin-Little (2002) note that it "usually lasts 3 or more years" (p. 42).

Although the lack of verbalizations is the primary symptom for this disorder, this symptom could reflect other problems as well. Dow and colleagues (1995) comment that the lack of verbalization may also be due to other factors, such as language deficits, "pervasive developmental disorder, schizophrenia, or another psychotic disorder" (p. 837). Therefore, a differential diagnosis (looking at potential diagnoses, ruling out those that do not fit the symptoms, and arriving at the most applicable diagnosis) is important so that appropriate intervention strategies can be implemented.

The Research

Investigators have explored the possible etiology of selective mutism. Dow and colleagues (1995) state that this disorder may be associated with shyness as well as with an introverted personality and affected by intrapsychic and social factors. These authors also report that, at times, selective mutism can be "associated with neuropsychological delays (developmental delays, speech and language disabilities, or difficulty processing social cues)" (p. 836).

If a child is very hesitant or has significant negative reactions to changes in routine or environment, he or she may display withdrawal (Drewes & Akin-Little, 2002). One way to withdraw is to avoid interacting verbally with those around you. Another possible explanation for selective mutism, according to Drewes & Akin-Little (2002), is that the symptoms emerge after the child experiences trauma or upset. This could be something as traumatic as physical assault or sexual abuse. It could also be an upsetting life event, such as the loss of a family member. According to Drewes & Akin-Little (2002), there is support for the assertion that anxiety is related to the presence of selective mutism and that some researchers suggest that the mutism may actually be one symptom of a more general, underlying anxiety disorder.

The link between anxiety and selective mutism may gain support from the results of a study conducted by Kristensen and Torgersen (2001). They found that *parents* of children with this disorder have a tendency to be anxious themselves in social situations. This raises questions regarding the connection between anxiety and this disorder as well as the influence of genetic, biological, and environmental factors.

In regard to the question of whether the lack of verbalizations that characterize children with selective mutism in particular settings is due to defiance or oppositionalism, Dow and colleagues (1995) report that recent speculation tends to favor the theory that anxiety, rather than oppositionalism, is at the root of selective mutism. Drewes and Akin-Little (2002) concur that future findings may not support the view that oppositionalism is associated with selective mutism, although they comment that each child must be looked at individually, because some children with this disorder may display the mutism because of underlying anxiety and others because of oppositionalism. In my experience, the majority of children I have encountered with selective mutism also had feelings of anxiety. However, there have been times when the mutism appeared to be symptomatic of a youngster suppressing anger (having the sensation of anger but not expressing it) toward a particular individual or environment.

Suggestions for Teachers: Helping Students with Selective Mutism

How can the teacher react to a child who refuses or is unable to speak in class because of selective mutism? First, it is important to find out which situations elicit this verbal constriction and in which situations the child feels more comfortable speaking. If the child is at ease speaking with adults but does not speak directly to other students, it may be helpful to initially have the child share information with the teacher in the presence of classmates. Some children with this difficulty respond well to immediate verbal reinforcement for speaking, but others feel self-conscious and uncomfortable with this reinforcement. Therefore, it is important to know the particular child's needs and desires. Parents may be a good source of information in attempting to understand the student.

If the child continues to be nonverbal in class, despite attempts at classroom support and close parent–teacher communication, the teacher might seek out the assistance of the school psychologist or discuss concerns with the building-level team of specialists. If typical strategies have not been successful, a thorough assessment of the child could include evaluations of many areas of functioning, especially because the symptom of mutism (not speaking) can be quite evident but the cause may not be. For instance, does the child hear the question? If not, it could explain why he or she failed to respond. Does the child understand the language? If not, perhaps finding someone who speaks the child's language and can translate information between student and classmates/teacher could initially be helpful as the child struggles to communicate and to feel competent in the classroom.

If the child is nonverbal at a certain point during the day, and it always corresponds with, say, math period, this would warrant further investigation. Is the child anxious about math class? But perhaps there is another reason, other than math, that leads to the lack of verbalizations during this period. For instance, if math class is the last period before lunch, perhaps the student is hypoglycemic. This may lead to lack of energy (e.g., motivation) to participate actively. The multidisciplinary approach to assessment can look at the many factors impacting a youngster with selective mutism.

Behavioral Interventions for Selective Mutism.

According to Stone and colleagues (2002), behavioral interventions are often helpful in treating this disorder. Drewes and Akin-Little (2002) state that behavioral techniques can be the most effective way of treating selective mutism. Behavioral interventions can include both positive and negative reinforcement. This may involve having a child practice speaking, which then results in the child receiving positive consequences. The therapist may also encourage the child to practice speaking and then reflect back to the youngster that no negative consequences resulted from the verbalizations. One behavioral technique highlighted by Drewes and Akin-Little (2000) is "stimulus fading" (p. 42).

Stimulus fading was used to help Dana. Dana's mother joined the class on a trip and accompanied her to some extracurricular social activities that involved large groups. Over time, Dana spoke with others in front of her mother. When her mother started to move away, or fade, from the situation, Dana maintained her verbalizations even without her mother's immediate presence. Eventually, Dana spoke to others without her mother being in the building.

Many of the behavioral techniques can be incorporated into a child's classroom setting with minimal disruption to the other children. If a teacher feels that such intervention is needed, it may be helpful to enlist the assistance of the building mental health professional and the parent to design a program that is suitable to the presenting symptoms and the child's individual needs. At times, treatment outside of school, such as psychotherapy or medication, may also be added to a particular child's intervention plan.

AUTISM AND ASPERGER'S DISORDER

Since autism and Asperger's disorder share some of the same diagnostic criteria, they are both explored in this section. First the criteria and characteristics of autism are reviewed.

Defining Autism

Autism has been defined as "a developmental disorder" that includes significant impairment in numerous areas, including "affective contact, abnormalities in social behavior, poor verbal and nonverbal communicative abilities, impairment in imaginative abilities, and a restricted range of interests" (Minshew, Goldstein, & Siegel, 1995, p. 255).

O'Riordan, Plaisted, Driver, and Baron-Cohen (2001) describe autism as follows:

> Autism is a psychiatric disorder that is characterized by three main features. The first feature encompasses gross social deficits, such as difficulties in forming and maintaining social relationships and deficits in engaging in reciprocal social interaction. The second defining characteristic of autism is a striking impairment in both verbal and nonverbal communication, . . . and the third component of this diagnostic triad is the presence of repetitive behavior. (p. 719)

According to Smith and Bryson (1994), some autistic children may not demonstrate the same level of impairment as others who have the same diagnosis. In regard to social difficulties exhibited by those with autism, Waterhouse, Fein, and Modahl (1996) reviewed the literature and report that the "lack of normal social affiliation" has been proposed to be related to "some other impairment," such as "information processing . . . executive function . . . language . . . attention . . . memory . . . and theory of mind" (p. 457), yet there is no evidence that these factors are causally related. Smith and Bryson (1994) report that difficulties in social relatedness may take a variety of forms, such as "aloof indifference to social ineptitude and inability to comprehend the viewpoints of others" (p. 259).

In regard to language communication skills, Minshew and colleagues (1995) note that, in more severe cases, the autistic youngster may be completely mute, although some level of speech is present in about 50 percent of those diagnosed. Mishew and colleagues (1995) studied the speech of those who were identified as having high-functioning autism. Based on the findings, these authors state that "autism may be a generalized disorder of complex information processing." Their results show that "mechanical and procedural language abilities," which may include such operations as defining concrete words and understanding grammatical and syntactical structure, do not show significant impairments. However, these same authors found that "interpretative language abilities," which are less concrete and require interpretation, are severely impaired (pp. 258–259).

Smith and Bryson (1994) reviewed some of the literature on autism and note that those with less severe forms of autism may struggle to use language for interpersonal communication, even while their formal language (e.g., ability to follow grammatical rules) may be accurate or even adhered to in an obsessive manner.

Some symptoms of autism must be present before a child reaches the age of 3 and must impact "at least one of the following areas . . . social interaction, . . . language as used in social communication, or . . . symbolic or imaginative play" (APA, 2000, p. 75). The disabling impact of the disorder depends on the severity of symptoms.

IAN: SEVERE AUTISM

Nine-year-old Ian was diagnosed with severe autism. He wore a helmet to prevent self-injuries from his repetitive attempts at head banging, he was generally nonverbal, and he was aggressive (e.g., hitting, pushing) if he experienced frustration. Ian was in a special education classroom that specialized in programs for autistic children with Ian's level of needs. His academic lessons included work on maintaining eye contact, using pictures to communicate his thoughts, and working on building a basic verbal vocabulary. Although there were other students in the classroom, his teacher reported that he never engaged in interactive play.

JOSH: MILD AUTISM

Josh is a 9-year-old boy diagnosed with mild autism. He is verbal and is generally interested in watching the other children interact in his mainstream classroom setting, but he has difficulty understanding some of the verbal abstract bantering and comments that classmates make to one another. Josh displays some obsessive characteristics (e.g., insisting that the teacher stick to a rigid schedule and not vary it for any reason) and stereotyped movements (e.g., hand flapping when he becomes nervous or overstimulated). With the assistance of an aide to guide him through the day, Josh is able to do much of the mainstream academic work.

Defining Asperger's Disorder

Without looking into Josh's developmental history, he may fit the overall criteria for Asperger's disorder. Some consider Asperger's disorder to be a mild form of autism (Perlman, 2000; Semrud-Clikeman & Hynd, 1990), although others report that they are "distinct syndrome(s)" (Semrud-Clikeman & Hynd, 1990). According to the American Psychiatric Association (2000), individuals should be diagnosed with Asperger's disorder only if they do not meet the criteria for autism. One differentiating factor, noted by the American Psychiatric Association (2000), is that "in contrast to Autistic Disorder, there are no clinically significant delays in early language" for those with Asperger's disorder (p. 81). Minshew and colleagues (1995) state that a difference between Asperger's disorder and autism lies in the history of early language development rather than in the particular ways that language is displayed later on in life. Due to Josh's history of significant delays in acquisition of early language skills, he would actually not meet the diagnostic criteria set forth above for this disorder, despite displaying symptoms that often characterize those with Asperger's.

The American Psychiatric Association (2000) states that "the essential features of Asperger's Disorder are severe and sustained impairment in social interaction . . . and the development of restricted, repetitive patterns of behavior, interest, and activities" (p. 80). Perlman (2000) reports that those with Asperger's disorder often have difficulty feeling empathy and "are generally unaware of the strangeness of their social presentation (i.e., they lack self-consciousness in the sense of being able to see themselves from another's point of view)" (p. 222).

In regard to their verbal communication, Perlman (2000) comments that these individuals may communicate with others about specific topics that they enjoy discussing, yet they may have difficulty sustaining a conversation about other topics and may try to return to the favored topic, often in a perseverative fashion, or withdraw from the discussion. Perlman notes that such individuals "may use words in odd ways and have equally idiosyncratic postural or gestural accompaniments to their speech. They seem to lack a sense of humor in that they do not understand subtle jokes" (p. 222).

Individuals with Asperger's disorder can be viewed as different or atypical in the ways in which they socialize and converse with others (Attwood, 1998; Perlman, 2000). As they get older, they may become depressed and socially withdrawn because they begin to recognize that they are somewhat different from those around them (Perlman, 2000).

Suggestions for Teachers: Helping Students with Autism or Asperger's Disorder

If a student with either autism or Asperger's disorder is in a mainstream classroom setting, it would be important for the teacher to understand the youngster's symptoms as well as his or her overall personality and abilities. Former teachers, parents, and special education staff may be able to help explain some of the needs that the child will have in the classroom. Fostering peer interactions in which the identified child encounters successful social experiences is an important part of many intervention strategies for children with Asperger's disorder, since they may struggle to understand their social world. Offering the student key phrases to use to enter into a discussion with peers or key comments that might be well received by others (e.g., "I really like the poster you made") may make it easier for that youngster to receive positive reinforcement for attempts at socialization.

In addition, the classroom teacher might monitor the student's understanding of abstract lessons and metaphorical comments; help the child to appropriately verbalize questions, answers, and thoughts; and even conduct a minilesson for all the students on conflict resolution (most students could probably benefit from such a lesson) so that the child with Asperger's disorder can learn the behaviors that are expected in the particular school setting. More individualized recommendations may come from the special education committee or from those who directly assist the student with his or her areas of need and strength.

LISA AND EVAN: AUTISTIC? SUFFERING FROM ASPERGER'S DISORDER?

Let us return to the case illustrations of Lisa and Evan. Is it possible that both of these students have autism or Asperger's disorder? At times, high-functioning children with these disorders may not have a diagnosis upon entering public school. Therefore, if a teacher notices the symptom cluster described earlier, the possibility that autism or Asperger's disorder is present could be considered.

Lisa's sullen, withdrawn demeanor may be her way of withdrawing from a world that is confusing to her. She may not understand the social demands of peer interactions, or she may be preoccupied with her own fixation on a particular thought. Evan, who presents as more agitated and disruptive, may be calling out in class because of a lack of understanding of the inappropriateness of his actions. However, the brief symptom descriptions of Lisa and Evan do not immediately indicate the presence of either autism or Asperger's disorder. Their behaviors may be due to other difficulties that were described earlier in this book. Any evaluator who administers a comprehensive assessment of either Lisa or Evan would need to consider the possibility of these disorders if the developmental, medical, social, academic, cognitive, and language factors are characteristic of either autism or Asperger's disorder.

TICS AND TOURETTE'S DISORDER

Many teachers have observed repetitive vocalizations or physical movements in children, such as throat clearing or eye blinking, when they have a sore throat or burning eyes due to allergies or a lack of adequate sleep. These repetitive behaviors may also reflect a student's nervousness or attempt to hold back tears. However, these same actions and others (e.g., repetitive facial movements and repetitive vocalizations such as grunting) may also indicate the presence of a tic or Tourette's disorder.

Defining Tics and Tourette's Disorder

The American Psychiatric Association (2000) states that "a tic is a sudden, rapid, recurrent, nonrhythmic, stereotyped motor movement or vocalization" (p. 108). It is "experienced as irresistible but can be suppressed for varying lengths of time. . . . Tics may be exacerbated during periods of stress" (p. 109). I have observed tics in children with many different stresses, including allergies, being overtired, having a fight with a friend, being nervous about a test in class, feeling physically ill, and having an adult reprimand them for displaying the initial symptoms.

Tourette's disorder is "characterized by multiple motor and vocal tics. The tics vary over time in both frequency and character and may include complex involuntary motor and vocal tics, copralalia, spitting, kicking, hitting, and other unusual gyrations" (Stebbins et al., 1995, p. 329). Shucard, Benedict, Tekok-Kilic, and Lichter (1997) note that the tics are "recurrent," "involuntary," and "interfere with daily function" (p. 147).

There appears to be a higher incidence of Tourette's disorder in the families of those diagnosed with the disorder (Schultz et al., 1998; Swerdlow, Magulac, Filion, & Zinner, 1996). Yeates and Bornstein (1994) report that symptoms of this disorder usually begin to emerge in childhood. The American Psychiatric Association (2000) criteria for this diagnosis includes persistent symptoms for a period greater than 12 months, although there may be brief periods when the child does not display the tics.

BENJAMIN: TOURETTE'S DISORDER

Six-year-old Benjamin has Tourette's disorder. At the start of the schoolyear, his first-grade teacher, Mr. Milton, noted that Benjamin frequently disrupted his classmates by "making noises," pulling the hair of other students, and making faces while Mr. Milton was teaching whole-group lessons. Before Benjamin's symptoms were fully understood, the school tried various ways of responding to his behaviors. Mr. Milton spoke with him in class about his actions and offered positive comments whenever Benjamin contributed in a positive fashion to the classroom activities. When these strategies did not lead to fewer disruptive behaviors, Benjamin was sent to the principal's office when he displayed actions that interfered with the other students' abilities to concentrate and learn. The principal tried to befriend Benjamin and to remind him of the reason for the school rules.

After Benjamin's fifth visit to the office, the principal and Mr. Milton met to review his difficulties. Both the principal and Mr. Milton felt that sending Benjamin to the principal was not effective. In fact, Benjamin generally displayed increased behavioral disruptions immediately following his return from the principal's office. The principal informed Mr. Milton that Benjamin's kindergarten teacher had noticed similar behaviors the previous year but had attributed them to immaturity. At this point, the principal and Mr. Milton agreed that it was important for Mr. Milton to have a conference with Benjamin's parent to determine the best way to proceed. Mr. Milton arranged a meeting with Benjamin's mother for the following week.

Benjamin's mother informed Mr. Milton that she had six children and that Benjamin often made "noises and faces at home just to get extra attention." She commented that she would like help to find ways to let Benjamin feel that he could get attention in a more positive fashion. She agreed to meet with the school's social worker that same day. Benjamin's mother informed the social worker that several of Benjamin's siblings also made "noises and faces" and that their teachers had spoken with her about these actions during each schoolyear. Upon further inquiry by the social worker, Benjamin's mother commented that her husband laughs when she complains about these behaviors and once informed her that he also made such noises and facial gestures when he was younger, but that it was "no big deal. I grew out of it."

The social worker invited Benjamin to join his mother in their meeting. Benjamin openly discussed the problematic behaviors. He seriously reported that "I can't really help it. Kids sometimes tease me about it. I don't like it, but I can't help it." It was at this point that the social worker began to suspect that Benjamin might be suffering from Tourette's disorder. He displayed the history of chronic tics, he reported that they were not purposeful actions, and the family history also lent support to this diagnosis.

The social worker spoke privately to Benjamin's mother about the disorder and questioned whether it might explain Benjamin's difficulties. Later, after a neurological evaluation, Benjamin was diagnosed with the disorder and began a treatment program. One component of Benjamin's plan involved allowing him to take a special pass from the teacher's desk and leave the room whenever he felt that he was struggling to contain noises. Benjamin would then take 5 minutes to go to the bathroom, where he let himself make the noises. When he returned to class, he was better able to concentrate on his classwork. Benjamin felt that the passes gave him greater control over his symptoms.

In addition, after speaking with Benjamin's neurologist and parents, Mr. Milton gave the other students a brief education about tics and communicated his expectation that the other students would respect Benjamin and his struggle with the disorder. Benjamin's neurologist also instituted a trial of medication.

These combined interventions led to gradual improvements in Benjamin's focus on academic work, since he was no longer preoccupied with his symptoms. His self-esteem also improved since the other students (and his mother) now understood his difficulties. In addition, Benjamin was relieved that he did not have to meet with the principal about his Tourette's-related behaviors; he was aware that his anxiety during those meetings had often created a greater need to make the Tourette's-related vocalizations.

Other Possible Difficulties Associated with Tourette's Disorder

While tics, such as those exhibited by Benjamin, are the main diagnostic features of Tourette's disorder, Swerdlow and colleagues (1996) reviewed the literature and report that "studies of neuropsychological function and psychophysiological performance in Tourette's disorder (TD) have identified deficits in attention, visuospatial perception, sensorimotor inhibition, and motor function" (p. 485). Schultz and colleagues (1998) note that it is not uncommon for children with Tourette's to have penmanship weaknesses that significantly affect school functioning. Tourette's disorder can be associated with symptoms of obsessive thoughts and compulsive behaviors and is found in some children with attention-deficit hyperactivity disorder, according to the American Psychiatric Association (2000).

Suggestions for Teachers: Helping Students with Tics or Tourette's Disorder

In the classroom, some students may feel embarrassed, socially isolated, and rejected and also experience low self-esteem because of their vocal and motor tics. The tics may be subtle (e.g., minor shoulder shrugs) or may be quite obvious and disruptive to the teacher's lesson (e.g., a loud laugh). A teacher who suspects that a child's actions may be due to a tic should consult with the school nurse and the child's parents to further explore this issue. However, there are numerous reasons why a child may exhibit a tic-like action, and not all such behaviors are reflective of Tourette's disorder or a chronic tic condition. Physiological causes and acute, short-term reactions to situational stress are just two possible reasons why these symptoms might be displayed. Depending on the diagnosis, the intervention plan may differ.

If a child with Tourette's disorder feels that the symptoms cannot be surpressed, it might be helpful to allow the child to periodically leave the classroom to go to the bathroom or to deliver a note to another teacher, thereby having more privacy to display the tic. These recommendations must be made with safety in mind. For instance, if a child's tic involves actions that may be seen as aggressive by others, it would be unfortunate if a fight broke out in the hallway because another child felt provoked by the student.

The supportive teacher—who confers with parents, shows respect for the child, and attempts to develop ways to manage the Tourette's symptoms— may help minimize the secondary difficulties the student may develop, such as depression, low self-esteem, and anxiety. If a management program or special education intervention is indicated, due to the level of impairment or disruption that the symptoms cause, the teacher may want to seek input from the school's mental health professionals, the school nurse, the school principal, the parent, and the student's doctor (if the parents approve of this contact). Depending on the child's level of self-awareness, teachers and parents may decide to consult him or her regarding what might help minimize subjective distress and how symptoms might be most easily managed.

PSYCHOSIS

Thompson and Havelkova (1983) note that a person diagnosed with psychosis has a marked distortion of reality, "affective responses" (p. 293) that are incongruent with a given situation, limited interpersonal relationships, and the inability to assume the responsibilities appropriate to one's age.

NICHOLAS: HEARING VOICES?

Seven-year-old Nicholas sits in class every day and appears to be motivated to do his work. He asks relevant questions to clarify his understanding of lessons and volunteers to contribute to classroom discussions. However, his teacher became concerned after noticing Nicholas mumbling to himself at certain points during the day. She suspected that Nicholas was hearing voices and nervously reported her suspicions to the building's assistant principal. Eventually, the school psychologist was consulted.

The school psychologist cautioned the teacher and assistant principal to avoid drawing conclusions before Nicholas's behavior could be more thoroughly understood. In this case, Nicholas was able to easily provide the answers when gently questioned about what he was saying when he was talking quietly to himself. Nicholas smiled and said, "I'm praying." His parents confirmed that Nicholas's behavior and the time of his quiet talk were consistent with praying.

Another child with Nicholas's symptoms may be talking to an imaginary friend, which is not necessarily abnormal for young children, or may be doing so because of a host of other reasons (e.g., a shy child's way of trying to talk to others or a medical difficulty such as a hearing problem).

Hallucinations

However, there are times when a child is experiencing hallucinations; these hallucinations may take the form of voices in one's head and the student may be responding to those voices.

There are many kinds of hallucinations. West (1987) notes that a person's hallucination may be "visual, auditory, olfactory, gustatory, tactile, kinesthetic, etc." (p. 51). West further comments that "the most frequent types of hallucinations are relatively undifferentiated: murmuring or buzzing sounds in the ears; flashing of light or darting movements in the periphery of vision; faint, unfamiliar odors; a slight, unpleasant taste in the mouth" (p. 51). These signs, however, do not necessarily indicate psychosis; in fact, many people may have had some similar experiences due to such factors as medical issues or simply everyday atypical experiences. Therefore, these more common causes would need to be ruled out before psychosis is diagnosed. Regarding hallucinations, West adds that "auditory hallucinations are the most common" and "voices, whether friendly or hostile, familiar or unfamiliar, are the most common specific manifestation" (p. 51).

Other Psychotic Symptoms

There are many ways in which psychotic symptoms can be manifested. These may include a student's perception of the surroundings that is not based on the shared reality of those nearby and perceptions that cannot be explained by cultural, religious, or other such factors. Psychotic symptoms may be secondary to a medical condition or to significant emotional distress, such as depression.

Suggestions for Teachers Who Suspect Psychosis

A teacher who believes that a child is psychotic should consult the building's team of specialists immediately—specifically, the mental health staff—before concluding that this is the case. The school psychologist, possibly with the input of a child psychiatrist, can determine what kind of assessment or intervention is indicated and whether the child is in a state of crisis. Psychotic symptoms should be taken seriously. Parents should be notified of the school's concerns, and the school may explore procedural, legal, and ethical guidelines for determining how to assure the student's safety and when to pursue a comprehensive evaluation. At times, a child may require such intensive intervention that hospitalization may be recommended until the crisis is addressed and the child is stable.

EATING DISORDERS—A BRIEF OVERVIEW

Many forms of eating problems can develop into disorders. Teachers have spoken with me about anorexia nervosa because of their concern about students who lose significant weight within a short period of time. Anorexia may be present if a person becomes significantly underweight, has a distorted view of him- or herself as still needing to lose weight, and has significant anxiety about regaining weight (APA, 2000).

On the other hand, a student with bulimia nervosa may not display significant weight loss. Instead, a student with this disorder may binge eat and then seek ways to avoid weight gain. Some youngsters make themselves throw up, while others use methods such as laxatives.

In my experience, both of these disorders are far more common in adolescents but not unknown in younger students. In regard to both anorexia and bulimia, there may be medical difficulties that mimic the symptoms. Therefore, it is important for the identified child to receive a comprehensive evaluation to determine the cause of the eating abnormalities. Both disorders can sometimes lead to significant physical complications and impairment—even death—so it is important for youngsters with eating disorders to be identified and provided with the appropriate assistance.

OTHER DISORDERS

There are numerous conditions and disorders that can impact children, such as drug/alcohol abuse, pica (eating nonfood items), stuttering, sleep disorders, enuresis/encopresis (wetting/soiling), those already noted in this book, and so forth. Because of the multitude of behaviors and emotions that can be symptomatic of difficulties in children, it is important for teachers to remind themselves that they are not working in isolation—mental health staff, learning specialists, administrators, speech pathologists, occupational therapists, physical therapists, medical consultants, and, most of all perhaps, parents and children can offer input into the appropriate classroom response to the child's needs and into whether additional evaluation or intervention is indicated.

THE ATYPICAL CHILD—NOT ALL CHILDREN ARE DISORDERED!

The good news is that children differ from one another. This means that a teacher will rarely have the same class atmosphere twice in a career. It means that society will probably not remain stagnant and students will look at the world through their own unique vantage points and potentially find ways to improve their environment and make a positive impact on others. The atypical child, who doesn't follow the trend but rather creates it, may eventually challenge our established ways of thinking and allow all of us to continue to grow and learn.

Some atypical students seem to have a disorder. They may be quiet, they may be challenging, or they may appear to be obsessed with certain ideas or topics. However, there are many children with these characteristics who are neither disordered nor impaired. A child from another culture may react differently from peers to certain lessons and activities. This youngster may display actions that are not typical of the group.

A child who is uniquely talented in an area may focus energy into the further development of the particular skill because it is both rewarding and exciting. With such a child, the classroom teacher may need to be creative in offering support for the area of giftedness and also in encouraging the student to include other topics into his or her educational experience.

Some children may be mislabeled as oppositional when they are truly just inquisitive and like to understand the rationale behind lessons. Such a student may question the validity of a concept or express questions about why the teacher is spending time teaching particular material. The interaction between teacher and student may determine how successful the year is for both—can a compromise be arranged? Perhaps the student can ask questions at a specific time during the day or be part of the planning of a lesson.

Students who appear to have a learning disability may instead have a learning preference. If a child tends to learn best through touch and movement, it may be more difficult for that youngster to easily understand lessons when they are presented verbally and the student is expected to sit at a desk and listen. A good match between teaching style and learning style can make a positive difference in the ease in which a youngster learns.

A student's temperament, desires, needs, and skills will all impact that youngster's behavior and availability to learn in a particular classroom. Teachers who can appreciate each child's uniqueness can then try to find the best fit between the student's personal style, the needs of the entire class, and the academic work that must be covered. Educators have reported that this process can be viewed as a rewarding journey for both student and teacher.

CONCLUSION

In conclusion, this chapter briefly addressed selective mutism, autism and Asperger's disorders, tics and Tourette's disorder, psychosis, eating disorders, and a few additional disorders and concluded with a discussion of how atypical children may not necessarily be abnormal or disordered. If a teacher is uncertain as to whether a student is atypical or suffering from a disorder, the best advice is to get to know the student. See how he or she thinks, feels, and learns. Gather information from those who have a history with the child. Then seek the advice of the building's specialists if concerns remain. However, in the case of a perceived crisis or dangerous situation, the child's teacher should immediately consult the specialists since time is of the essence.

REFERENCES

American Psychiatric Association (APA). (2000). *Diagnostic and statistical manual of mental disorders: Fourth edition, DSM-IV-TR, text revision.* Washington, DC: Author.

Attwood, T. (1998). *Asperger's syndrome*. Philadelphia: Jessica Kingley Publishers.

Dow, S. P., Sonies, B. C., Schieb, D., Moss, S. E., & Leonard, H. L. (1995). Practical guidelines for the assessment and treatment of selective mutism. *Journal of the American Academy of Child and Adolescent Psychiatry, 34*(7), 836–846.

Drewes, K. M., & Akin-Little, A. (2002). Children with selective mutism: Seen but not heard. *The School Psychologist, 56*(2), 37, 40–42, 54–55, 65.

Kristensen, H., & Torgersen, S. (2001). MCMI-II personality traits and symptom traits in parents of children with selective mutism: A case-control study. *Journal of Abnormal Psychology, 110*(4), 648–652.

Minshew, N. J., Goldstein, G., & Siegel, D. J. (1995). Speech and language in high-functioning autistic individuals. *Neuropsychology, 9*(2), 255–261.

O'Riordan, M. A., Plaisted, K. C., Driver, J., & Baron-Cohen, S. (2001). Superior visual search in autism. *Journal of Experimental Psychology: Human Perception and Performance, 27*(3), 719–730.

Perlman, L. (2000). Adults with Asperger disorder misdiagnosed as schizophrenic. *Professional Psychology: Research and Practice, 31*(2), 221–225.

Schultz, R. T., Carter, A. S., Gladstone, M., Scahill, L., Leckman, J. F., Peterson, B. S., Zhang, H., Cohen, D. J., & Pauls, D. (1998). Visual-motor integration functioning in children with Tourette's syndrome. *Neuropsychology, 12*(1), 134–145.

Semrud-Clikeman, M., & Hynd, G. W. (1990). Right hemispheric dysfunction in nonverbal learning disabilities: Social, academic, and adaptive functioning in adults and children. *Psychological Bulletin, 107*(2), 196–209.

Shucard, D. W., Benedict, R. H. B., Tekok-Kilic, A., & Lichter, D. G. (1997). Slowed reaction time during a continuous performance test in children with Tourette's syndrome. *Neuropsychology, 11*(1), 147–155.

Smith, I. M., & Bryson, S. E. (1994). Imitation and action in autism: A critical review. *Psychological Bulletin, 116*(2), 259–273.

Stebbins, G. T., Singh, J., Weiner, J., Wilson, R. S., Goetz, C. G., & Gabrieli, J. D. E. (1995). Selective impairments of memory functioning in unmedicated adults with Gilles de la Tourette's syndrome. *Neuropsychology, 9*(3), 329–337.

Stone, B. P., Kratochwill, T. R., Sladezcek, I., & Serlin, R. C. (2002). Treatment of selective mutism: A best-evidence synthesis. *School Psychology Quarterly, 17*(2), 168–190.

Swerdlow, N. R., Magulac, M., Filion, D., & Zinner, S. (1996). Visuospatial priming and latent inhibition in children and adults with Tourette's disorder. *Neuropsychology, 10*(4), 485–494.

Thompson, M., & Havelkova, M. (1983). Psychosis in childhood and adolescence. In P. D. Steinhauer & Q. Rae-Grant (Eds.), *Psychological problems of the child in the family (2nd ed.)* (pp. 293–294). New York: Basic Books.

Waterhouse, L., Fein, D., & Modahl, C. (1996). Neurofunctional mechanisms in autism. *Psychological Review, 103*(3), 457–489.

West, L. J. (1987). The meaning of hallucinations. In F. Flach (Ed.), *Diagnostics and psychopathology* (pp. 49–52). New York: Norton.

Yeates, K. O., & Bornstein, R. A. (1994). Attention deficit disorder and neuropsychological functioning in children with Tourette's syndrome. *Neuropsychology, 8*(1), 65–74.

CHAPTER 8

A Positive Journey Through Elementary School

Students, Parents, and Teachers Offer Words of Advice

In this chapter, students and former students describe how an elementary school teacher made a positive impact on their development. I have found that children can sometimes be the most innocent, yet most informative, teachers. They have firsthand knowledge of life with a challenge and know what made them feel more successful in school.

Parents and experienced educators also offer suggestions on how certain teaching strategies may benefit children with particular areas of difficulty. While I have quoted each person directly, pseudonyms are used to protect confidentiality.

STUDENTS SPEAK UP

Mike: ADHD and Giftedness

This young man is just a few years out of elementary school and has a clear memory of activities that helped him to feel comfortable in the classroom. Mike has been identified as both gifted and as suffering from an attention-deficit hyperactivity disorder (ADHD).

> I am in eighth grade and I really haven't liked school, but a few teachers have been able to help me. I will tell you how one, my second-grade teacher, made it fun for me.
>
> I hate it when teachers just read out facts. It is so boring. My second-grade teacher had spunk and didn't talk in [a] monotone. She also had a lot of good ideas on fun things to do. We did "star of the week," which was show and tell.
>
> She also had great ways of teaching. We were learning mostly about the Renaissance, so we had a big festival and went to the real Renaissance festival. She also let us stay after and help her clean up and gave us some candy. I hope this helped you.

145

Mike highlights the fact that ADHD children often benefit from more interactive and less *passive* learning experiences. In addition, he expressed positive feelings about having been acknowledged as a valuable individual. As teachers try to cover the core content areas for the year, it is important not to lose sight of the special qualities that each student has to share.

Laura: Giftedness

This young-adolescent female does not have the "typical" challenges. She is gifted, and this level of intellectual functioning has presented some struggles for her during her educational career. Here are her words.

> When people talk about me as a "gifted child," I think of how I was bored in many of my classes. However, I don't remember being bored in fifth grade.
>
> My teacher had an amazing personality. I remember the dog that she was training. He was sent off to a man who had a disease and needed him. My teacher would tell us all about how the dog was doing and about each time that he saved the man's life.
>
> That wasn't the only thing I remember about her. My teacher also gave a few other students and myself different worksheets than the rest of the class sometimes, to challenge us. And there would always be an "extra-challenging" problem on the bottom of our math sheets. She also made parts of learning fun.
>
> Even if it was easy, my teacher made it fun. When we were learning geography in social studies, we made papier-mâché globes to help us remember the continents. We made up flashcards for our vocabulary words and got into groups or pairs to quiz each other. But the most special thing to me about my teacher was that she inspired me. I suppose I have been a writer all my life, but my fifth-grade teacher showed me my talent. She inspired me to write poems (I wrote one for Earth Day and read it over the PA system), short stories (I expressed my feelings for my dead cat in my first real short story), and helped me show my persuasive side in essays. My fifth-grade teacher has probably been the best teacher I had in elementary school.

When a teacher has a classroom full of students, it can sometimes be difficult to tailor work to each student. However, students seem to recognize the effort and, according to Laura, respond positively when a teacher helps to make the work personally meaningful to the learner. Laura also reported that activities (e.g., group projects) and being recognized for her strengths helped to make her school experience memorable.

Elliot: ADHD and Learning Disability

This young man has the benefit of being out of elementary school for many years and can use the wisdom of years in offering his input. This student suffered from ADHD and a learning disability.

> In second grade, my teacher put me on the side of the room closest to the door. I was able to get up, get a drink, and stretch my legs whenever I needed. In fifth grade, I remember I had to read a particular book. My teacher gave me a shorter chapter to review, and report on, than the other kids got. Also in fifth grade, my teacher asked me to come in 15 minutes earlier on Tuesday and Thursday mornings. She helped me to organize my desk and papers.
>
> My school district supplied me with a tape recorder. Each month, I received the books we had to read on tape. I listened to the tapes and read along at the same time.

Several comments are worth noting in this statement. ADHD children may have significant difficulty containing their physical energy in the traditional classroom. Because the student was allowed to move around within acceptable limits, he seemed to feel that his teacher recognized his difficulty and did not view him as a behaviorally disruptive student. In addition, ADHD students often struggle with organization. When the teacher asked Elliot to come to school early to organize his materials, he did not see this as a punishment, but rather as the teacher taking a personal interest in him and aiding him. When a teacher communicates a genuine desire to help, many students will see this and feel supported.

For Elliot, some academic modifications were also made due to his learning disability. If a general education teacher feels that a challenged student needs some modifications, it is advisable to discuss this issue with the school-based team of specialists and with the child's parent.

Glenn: Central Auditory–Processing Disorder

This individual has been diagnosed with a central auditory–processing disorder (CAPD). He is now a man and can reflect back on his public school career. Here are his words.

> For most of my educational and even pre-educational career, I was always pushed hard to do my work, but I never quite seemed to be able to reach my full potential. Nobody understood why. Eventually,

I was tested and found to have CAPD. Then, my problem began to make sense to me.

In school, my resource room teacher did not so much help me cope with my emotions about my disability, but she helped me tremendously work through my school work. She made the work easier by giving me encouragement and support and by helping me find ways around the problems. I began to feel less anxious and even began to enjoy school.

Making the final hurdle didn't come until later, when I began seeing a psychiatrist. Working with him, he helped me understand that it wasn't my fault. After realizing that, my grades and confidence shot up.

This young man benefited from knowledge about why, at times, learning was difficult for him. Some students can handle hearing about their disorder in elementary school, but others may not be emotionally ready to hear that something is wrong. Therefore, it is recommended that any information shared with a child about his or her learning style and challenges should occur after thoughtful exploration and parent–educator discussions about the possible advantages and disadvantages that this knowledge would have for the student. Sometimes a child is given a general description of how he or she might learn differently from the mainstream child, but this information should always be given along with a clear explanation about areas of strengths.

In the material just presented, it is apparent that some disabled students blame themselves for their problems or have significant emotional concerns because of their academic and learning experiences. These issues are ones that educators should watch out for and communicate to parents and school mental health staff, if noted.

Jeff: Giftedness and Learning Disability

This adult reflects on how it was to be a young student struggling with being gifted and learning disabled.

One of my schoolteachers took a special interest in me at a point in time where my loss of self-worth could have made my life much worse. He gave me projects to build, knowing that this was my area of strength. Another teacher somehow gave of himself by being supportive and reassuring. A third teacher helped me in nonstandard ways by giving me individual attention and help when I was struggling. Without these teachers' support, my self-esteem would have suffered even more than it did.

Jeff has emphasized the fact that it is so important, even essential, for students to feel valued, competent, and given emotional support so that they develop a sense of self-worth and can ultimately value their individual learning abilities.

PARENTS SPEAK UP

Marie: Son Diagnosed with a Learning Disability

In her own words, this parent describes her personal views about how certain interventions have been beneficial to her son.

> In second grade, my child's school difficulties surfaced. He was labeled as a disruptive child. Having raised him to respect others, I was shocked, hurt, and angry for someone to say such things of my little boy. That's when I insisted that there was a problem and had him tested.
>
> The school psychologist informed me that my son had a learning disability and assured me that any child with his difficulty would also stare out the window and be inattentive in school. He couldn't understand what the teacher was saying and he was bored.
>
> My son's problem was auditory. He couldn't follow verbal instructions. If you showed my son how to use something, rather than by telling him the instructions, he'd catch on right away. If the teacher used props for a lesson, that helped. My son always needed to have lessons written on the board in elementary school. If he could see/touch, then he had no problem. He's made a fabulous career utilizing these strengths.
>
> It was in third grade that he received the most important help for his new educational adventure. His third-grade special education teacher taught him the standard lessons, and she explained to me that the first lessons that she taught her children were self-respect and confidence. My son came home so happy from school those first days in this class. And he continued always to have that feeling of self-confidence. This third grade teacher was *the* teacher that gave my son his future.

I highly respect and am thankfully in debt to the wonderful teachers who helped my son throughout his schooldays. But most importantly, all parents must work very hard to support their children.

As an adult, my son is a wonderful, personable, people-person who enjoys life.

Marie has the benefit of knowing that her learning disabled child has grown into a happy, successful adult. In her statement, she reminds us that a child's overt behaviors (e.g., "He was labeled as a disruptive child") may not directly communicate the underlying reasons for symptoms. In this case, the frustration of struggling with an unidentified learning disability appears to have been a significant factor that led to the behavioral difficulties.

This parent also reinforces the fact that there are many ways to teach children, and even though her son struggled with auditory learning, he was quite capable of learning, particularly when the lessons emphasized visual and tactile methods of teaching. Finally, Marie restates what the children themselves reported earlier in this chapter—that one's self-concept and self-esteem are critical areas to help develop in all students.

Nancy: Daughter Diagnosed with ADHD and Motor Deficits

This parent does not yet have the benefit of watching her child grow into a happy adult. She has a young child who is just starting her formal school experience. Nancy describes her young daughter's challenges and how school programs and staff have helped make school a rewarding experience for both child and parent.

I am writing as a parent of a 5½-year-old child who struggles with an attention-deficit hyperactivity disorder in addition to gross motor and fine motor deficits. Although my daughter is just beginning the journey through elementary school, I have already observed the difference that a teacher can make in a child's motivation and interest in learning.

My child is currently participating in an inclusion class where there is collaboration among team members, including the general education teacher, special educator, and other support personnel. The teachers provide her with verbal reinforcers and visual prompting to extend her on-task attention. Peer modeling and praise are also effective. In addition, my daughter has shown growth in her self-esteem by being used as a peer model during activities that demonstrate her strengths. She is excited about school and is an active participant now rather than the reluctant observer she used to be.

I have found the behavioral intervention, which was in place the first day of school, to be a great benefit to my child. All of the children in the class participate in the behavioral intervention. Therefore, there is no obvious distinction between the children with special needs and their typical peers. This plan has benefited my child, since she is aware of what is expected of her, is aware of the consequences of her behavior, is actively participating in the reinforcement process, and has begun to reflect on her own behavior with less direct adult intervention.

With the input of the educational team, I have been able to develop strategies for improving my daughter's organizational skills and cooperation at home. For instance, through the use of sequencing our morning and evening routines, both visually and verbally, there is less rushing, anxiety, and frustration during times which were in the past extremely difficult due to my daughter's distractibility and inattentiveness. My husband and I have each taken activities provided by physical and occupational therapists to use in play with my daughter to enhance development of her motor skills and to encourage self-help and independence at home. This has reduced the level of stress and frustration in our home and created a more positive interaction between all family members.

Once again, the importance of building a child's self-esteem and emphasizing a student's strengths is mentioned. Nancy also presented numerous specific interventions that are typically used by teachers. Verbal reinforcement (e.g., "It was so nice to have you raise your hand today and give such an interesting comment"), visual prompts, behavior modification, and clear classroom expectations are often helpful tools for an educator to use with children with varied needs. In the next section, a teacher describes how she uses behavior modification in her class to help build a sense of community and to help all the young students.

TEACHERS SPEAK UP

Amy: Experienced Teacher and Staff Developer

Amy is an experienced educator and staff developer. In her written comments, Amy describes how she has used behavior modification in her classroom setting.

A good teacher knows that it is her job to reach every learner in her classroom in spite of the diverse learning community which may include an infinite combination of different types of learners. It is often this diversity that creates the greatest challenge to the classroom teacher. When one child's impulsivity disrupts the cadence of your delivery and another child is lost in thought as she stares out the window, the best planning efforts and teaching antics are thwarted. You know you are not reaching all of your children and you find yourself frustrated, asking, "How am I going to teach *all* of the children in this classroom?" The answer lies in good classroom management, and more specifically, behavior management.

Most teachers have at one time or another created a behavior-modification plan for an individual child. For example, if you have a child who chronically forgets her homework, you might create a sticker chart and, when she reaches her goal, reward her by sharing your lunchtime with her and two of her friends. Good classroom management employs the same tactics. A teacher determines the behaviors that lend themselves to the most productive educational environment and seeks ways to make them an integral part of the learning climate.

I always begin the year with the kids brainstorming a list of rewards that would be motivating to them yet cost-free to me. A sampling of things that have been on that list include extra recess, board game afternoon, and three nights of no homework. In order to earn one of these rewards, I start the year with a marble jar and try to catch kids "being good." Whenever I see a child sitting quietly, one with great listening posture, one who has followed the directive given, I plunk a marble into the jar. I am very generous with the marbles because my goal is to motivate and convey the message of what I perceive as good behavior.

As the year progresses, the novelty of the marble jar tends to wear off, so I change the venue. I might create a "star board" and use stickers to recognize the behaviors I am seeking—I look to my class to guide the decisions I make regarding functioning as a cohesive unit. In some instances, whole-class behavior modification loses its effectiveness altogether, in which case I will then try small-group strategies such as table sticker charts. Ultimately, what I seek to do is create that "optimal learning environment" where all children, in spite of their learning style, get the most out of each and every schoolday.

In this piece, the teacher describes several ways of instituting a behavior-modification program. It can be tailored to the needs of an individual child or to the needs of the entire classroom. There are many ways to administer a behavior-modification program, and the target goals may dictate which programs are better than others. When appropriate, children seem to enjoy being active participants in the development of the plan.

Some individuals may look negatively upon behavior-modification programs and comment that they are simply rewarding children for things that they should be expected to do anyway. In daily life, however, we are all responsive to a behavior-modification program. For instance, if a cashier in a supermarket always acts annoyed and tells us to hurry to pay because there is a long line of people waiting, many of us would avoid that person in the future. The child who tells the teacher, "You are the smartest person in the whole world," will certainly elicit a more positive response from the teacher than the cashier did from the customer. Our responses are shaped daily by those around us. In fact, many employees feel positive reinforcement each year when given a bonus check for working beyond the standard expectations. No matter how old any of us become, verbal praise and positive reinforcement will often leave us more motivated for the next activity. Hopefully, a behavior-modification program in the classroom will similarly create a positive learning attitude and environment for the students.

Danielle: Science Teacher and Mentor

This educator has extensive experience teaching science and mentoring educators.

> The influence that a teacher has in the lives of children can be considerable. Teachers can affect their love of a subject and, more importantly, their self-confidence. Students need to feel that teachers value them as well as their opinions. Respect in a classroom is a two-way street. If a student feels valued, teaching becomes pleasant and successful.
>
> It would be wonderful if all students had an equal ability to learn academic lessons, but this is just not so. Identifying learning problems can help the students by decreasing their frustration and increasing their self-confidence. It also helps control many discipline problems in the classroom. Finding a way to deal with the learning problem can result in student success.
>
> Accommodating a student who has difficulty reading by giving an oral exam, for instance, can allow that student to show that the subject matter has been learned. In this way, the test measures the amount of information learned without penalizing the student for the difficulties resulting from the reading disability. If you give a student a measure of success, it can "turn them on to learning." Encouragement works!

Teaching science has the benefit of "hands-on" experiences. Lab work allows the students to use equipment and discover for themselves the answers to problems. Working in groups can be both educationally and socially beneficial. Authentic learning can have many benefits for students. I taught meteorology by installing a weather station at my school. The lesson was incredibly successful.

Every student had an opportunity to take instrument readings, formulate a forecast, and announce it on the school's PA system. This established a real sense of importance and made the students enjoy a topic that could have been somewhat dry. Education, like everything else, is trial and error. When it works, it's great!

This teacher highlights the fact that a student's self-confidence is important to foster and that a child with learning difficulties may act-out in the classroom because of feelings of frustration. Danielle also notes that children do not all have the same learning style or abilities. The creative teacher learns how to teach in a way that allows varied learners to gain from the lessons. This teacher reinforces some statements made earlier in this chapter about the value of group projects and "authentic learning."

Jill: Special Education Teacher

Jill has extensive experience teaching special education and special-needs children. She offers a particular strategy that might help some learners.

Of help to young visual learners who are having difficulty reading is a system of color coding. One method I used with some of my students that proved helpful was to print the vowel in red, two consonants together in green (to suggest that the child should blend the sounds together), and purple was used to indicate that the letter or combination of letters could be a troublemaker (*oy* as in *boy* or *sch* as in *school*).

The system has been used successfully with both readers who are struggling with the decoding process as well as with those who are truly learning disabled. I have used individual notebooks for the children and/or put words on separate cards so that they might study them. The children enjoy drilling each other on the words. Often they will color code for their friends, which gives them added practice and makes their self-esteem take a step upward.

This color coding has limited application, but it can give some students a taste of success.

Jill highlights the fact that teachers can use creative methods of teaching to assist a child in developing reading skills and to emphasize a child's learning strengths. In this statement, the benefit of peer interactions was mentioned. This topic has repeatedly been raised in this chapter, suggesting that teachers do not need to be the only individuals in the classroom to teach and reinforce lessons. When group work, peer modeling, or peer interactions foster learning, many children will find this social/academic experience enjoyable. However, there is always the risk that the socially isolated child may be left out if children are encouraged to form their own groups. Therefore, teachers should consider this before encouraging children to select their work partners.

Helen: Special Educator

Helen is a special education teacher who summarizes areas that she believes are essential for new educators to remember when working with children like those in her own classroom.

> I am a special education teacher working with students classified as emotionally disturbed and mildly retarded. Some of the children have autistic-like qualities and ADHD. There are many challenges in teaching this population. I have found that my lessons must be short. The children lose interest and become easily distracted. Because of this, I often present the lesson to the whole group (15 minutes) and break into small groups to complete the activity (15 minutes) and then regroup to tie up the lesson (10 minutes). This seems to work because the students are only spending a short time on each part of the lesson.
>
> Another thing that I have found to work in teaching is using the multiple-intelligence theory. This theory suggests that people have different ways of "being smart" and learn through different media. Some of the intelligences I use are musical/rhythmic, visual/spatial, bodily/kinesthetic. These seem to be dominant areas for my students, and I found that if my lessons include activities in these areas, they are more successful.
>
> For musical/rhythmic, we will make up a rhyme or use a song to learn a new concept. For instance, the days of the week are sung to one song, while the alphabet song can be sung to a different tune. For the visual/spatial lesson, I use a lot of pictures, visual aids, or modeling. For the bodily/kinesthetic lesson, I try to incorporate movement, the use of manipulatives, and hands-on activities.

It's not always easy, and I've learned to adjust my style and try new things. If it works, great; if not, I'll try something else!

CONCLUSION

The benefits of flexibility in teaching and multisensory approaches to communicating information, as well as the many ways in which a child can show ability, are all repeatedly mentioned by educators who successfully reach special-needs children. In fact, these are sound principles for teachers of *all* children. Some children struggle to write a report about a book but can act out a part or verbally describe the story. Other children struggle to communicate verbally but can create a photo essay about a particular topic. Although teachers may be challenged by the uniqueness of how each child learns, the inherent diversity of their students can also be viewed as one of the most exciting parts of the teaching profession. No two students, no two classes, are identical.

KEY COMMENTS BY THE CONTRIBUTORS TO THIS CHAPTER

- It is extremely important to try to foster student self-confidence.
- Group interactions may help children.
- There are many ways to administer and many benefits to implementing behavior modification.
- There are benefits to using authentic learning and multisensory learning.
- Appreciating the special qualities (strength, weaknesses, and unique characteristics) of each student allows the educator to develop more effective lessons and to enjoy the unique contributions that students can offer to class discussions and classroom dynamics.

Index

About the Author

Dr. Moss has her doctorate in clinical psychology. She is a licensed psychologist, a certified school psychologist, a Diplomate in School Psychology through the American Board of Professional Psychology, and a Fellow in the American Academy of School Psychology. She specializes in child and family psychology. Dr. Moss has published within her field. She has also been on the editorial advisory board, and been a reviewer, for several publications.